Cybertraps for Educators

By Frederick S. Lane

~~~~~~~~

PUBLISHED BY

Frederick S. Lane

Cybertraps for Educators

Original Copyright 2015

Version

D1115722

Cover Design by Colin Gliech

On LinkedIn: http://www.linkedin.com/in/colingliech

Frederick S. Lane

License Notes for This E-Book

This e-book is licensed for your personal enjoyment only. This e-book may not be re-sold or given away to other people. If you would like to share this book with another person, please purchase an additional copy for each recipient. If you are reading this book and did not purchase it, or it was not purchased for you, then please visit your favorite online retailer and purchase your own copy. Thank you for respecting the hard work of the author.

~~~~~~~~~

Table of Contents

Section III: Cybertraps Involving Students

Section IV: Teacher Precautions and Solutions

~~~~~~~~

Introduction
From Slate to Tablet

For Educators, Administrators, and Parents

Few professions are as important, or as difficult, as teaching. I am fortunate to have a number of teachers in my family, and I am married to a professor of art history, so I have seen up close the day-to-day difficulty of educating students with variable interests, talents, challenges, and levels of maturity. Ten years of service as a Commissioner on the Burlington, VT School Board further underscored the complexity of educating students in an era of near-constant funding crises, political debates, and changing standards for assessment.

Without question, however, this tough job is getting steadily more difficult. For the last fifteen years or so, I have researched and written about the impact of technology on society. Three years ago, I wrote *Cybertraps for the Young*, which detailed the legal trouble that children can get into through the use and misuse of electronic devices, online services, and smartphone apps. During the course of writing that book, it became clear that technology was creating similar issues for teachers, school administrators, and even school board members.

The goal of this book is to help prospective, new, and seasoned educators better understand the potential challenges raised by technology, as well as the very real legal risks that can arise through its misuse and malicious application. To be clear, I am a big fan of digital technology, and firmly believe that its myriad benefits vastly outweigh the negative consequences. At the same time, however, we need to be realistic about the potential for abuse, and do everything possible to prevent students (and educators themselves) from becoming victims of cyberabuse. My hope is that this book will help educators reflect on their own use (or misuse) of technology, and advance the conversation about how best to offer students all of the advantages of technology while minimizing the potential risks.

Overview of the Contents

This initial edition of *Cybertraps for Educators* is divided into four main sections: 1) Cybertraps in the Workplace; 2) Cybertraps Outside the Workplace; 3) Student-Related Cybertraps; and 4) Teacher Precautions and Solutions. The following is a brief description of each section.

Cybertraps in the Workplace

This section covers cybertraps that educators may stumble into in their capacity as employees. They range from the relatively pedestrian and widespread issue of cyberloafing to the much more serious issue of receipt and possession of child pornography (which can of course occur outside of the workplace as well, but is a much more serious problem when it occurs on school property and through the use of school equipment).

Cybertraps Outside the Workplace

These cybertraps raise the issue of the perpetual tension between technology and privacy, particularly for public employees like teachers. The topics discussed range from protection of (or limitations on) a teacher's right to express his or her opinions, to whether a teacher should be allowed to use school equipment to advertise illegal services.

Student-Related Cybertraps

Teachers spend a lot of time in close contact with tech-savvy (and tech-crazed) students. Technology is playing a leading role in a number of serious potential student-related cybertraps, ranging from cyberbullying and cyberbaiting to sexual assault. This section offers some case studies to illustrate the various potential risks.

Teacher Precautions and Solutions

This section suggests steps that teachers can take to minimize their risk of falling into the various cybertraps discussed in the book, as well as steps that they can take to improve the safety of everyone in their district.

Throughout this book, I've drawn on incidents and case studies from a variety of different countries. The bulk of the examples are drawn from the United States, but there are also stories of teachers who have run into trouble in Canada, the United Kingdom, and Australia. What I hope this will illustrate is that the cybertraps faced by educators are increasingly global in nature, given the worldwide reach of the Internet and the universality of both hardware and software. No educational system—and no educator—is completely risk-free when it comes to the temptations and tribulations of our technological age.

~~~~~~~~~

Section One
Cybertraps in the Workplace

"I hope there's somebody out there who realizes that I haven't done anything different from what most teachers would do. There will be teachers out there thinking: 'There but for the grace of God'."—Sian Mediana, Welsh elementary school teacher, reflecting on her disciplinary proceeding for allegedly surfing the Web on personal business during school hours.[1.1]

~~~~~~~~~

Frederick S. Lane

Chapter One
Cyberloafing

Very few of us can honestly say that we haven't lost the odd hour or two (or forty) online. Facebook, Buzzfeed, Twitter, Pinterest, DailyKos, xkcd, *The Huffington Post, The New York Times, The Boston Globe* sports page—the cyber universe is filled with enticing and time-consuming distractions. A random walk around the Internet is not a problem on a lazy Sunday morning or even a slightly-depressing Saturday night home alone, but it's a much bigger deal when someone is supposed to actually be working.

Employers of every description are deeply concerned about the impact of the Internet on productivity, and with good reason. In HR circles, the phenomenon even has a new name: "cyberloafing" (which is marginally preferable to the more judgmental "cyberslacking"). By some estimates, cyberloafing costs the American economy billions of dollars every year in lost productivity. According to Kansas State University Associate Professor Joseph Ugrin, "the average US worker spends 60-80 per cent of their time online at work doing things unrelated to their jobs."[1,2]

Even before Facebook was widely available (the site did not become generally accessible by the public until September 2006), a study by the Internet firm Websense found that 62 percent of men and 54 percent of women accessed the Web during the workday for personal reasons.[1.3] By contrast, *Forbes* contributor Cheryl Connor reported in 2013 that while the percentage of cyberloafers had risen only slightly (to 64 percent), social media sites were a significant part of the problem. "The winners for the time-loss warp," Connor said, "are Tumblr (57%), Facebook (52%), Twitter (17%), Instagram (11%), and SnapChat (4%)."[1.4]

The concern over cyberloafing has helped fuel a multi-billion dollar workplace surveillance industry. Employers, including school districts, have implemented a staggering array of surveillance tools, from monitoring software to closed-circuit cameras to location-based tracking (GPS, RFID, swipe cards, and the soon-to-be ubiquitous iBeacon[1.5]). There are multiple reasons for such surveillance, of course, particularly in schools; cameras, swipe cards, and other tools are all integral to protecting students and staff. But there is no question that the mix of employee cyberloafing and employer efforts to prevent it has had a toxic effect on workplace morale and employee privacy.

The vast majority of teachers have less obvious opportunities to goof around on the Internet than many other types of employees who spend the bulk of their days on computers. It's enough of a challenge simply to ride herd on 20, 30, or even more students, while at the same time providing meaningful instruction on substantive topics. Nonetheless, a surprising number of teachers find time to surf the Web when they're supposed to be working, and cyberloafing is often listed as a good way to lose a teaching job.[1.6]

Take, for example, the case of Sian Mediana, an elementary school teacher at the Fairwater primary school in Cardiff, Wales. A four-day investigation at the school revealed that Mediana's computer had been used to visit a variety of non-work-related Web sites, including Lloyds.com (banking), eBay, and Friends Reunited (a British social networking site). One of Mediana's teaching assistants, Karen Lawrence, testified at a hearing of the General Teaching Council of Wales, and said that her colleague would surf the Web 2-3 hours per day. [1.7]

"If she sold something on eBay," Lawrence said, "we would turn it into activity for the children and take them with us to the Post Office. [Mediana] would also look at financial sites and talk to us about it during work." [1.8]

Although she resigned from the Fairwater school following the in-house investigation, Mediana strenuously contested the charges at the GTCW hearing, saying that while she did check her bank accounts and purchase school books on eBay, she never did so during school hours. She also suggested that her teaching assistants were simply lying about the amount of time she spent online, and that other teachers (including her assistants) might have been responsible for the non-school activity. However, IT specialists found that all of the activity was specific to Mediana's computer and her password.

Teaching Council solicitor Damian Phillips summed up the evidence by stating that "It is wholly unreasonable to believe other teachers were coming in during teaching hours, logging on to the Internet using her computer and her identity."[1.9]

The General Teaching Council ultimately found Mediana guilty of unprofessional conduct, but said that she could return to teaching so long as she only used school computers for professional purposes, and alerted any prospective headmasters of the disciplinary order. In the months following the hearing, however, Mediana was unable to find a new position, and told a reporter that she regretted submitting her resignation.[1.10]

"I should never have resigned," Mediana said, "because I don't think I would have lost my job over this. I was told if I resigned it would all be over with."[1.11]

From one perspective, teachers who surf the Web during class time are committing the same offense as any other bored employee; they're not doing what they're being paid to do. That alone is sufficient grounds for school districts and school boards to be concerned and take disciplinary action. But a lack of focus and attention is more dangerous in the classroom than it is in the average office, since teachers are responsible for the supervision and well-being of their students.

The potential dangers were illustrated by the 2009 case of Thomas McCoy, a teacher at the Royal Palm Exceptional Center, an alternative school for special needs students in Fort Myers, Florida. While McCoy was supposedly supervising four students, another of the school's employees walked by the classroom and saw a female student performing a sex act on a male student behind a bookcase. The employee also told district officials that she saw McCoy using a computer with his back to the bookcase. Computer forensic analysis of the computer's browser history showed that at the time the incident between the students took place, McCoy was surfing the ESPN.com Web site.[1.12] Six months later, McCoy was terminated by the School Board of Lee County.[1.13]

As I noted at the start, most teachers are so busy that it's almost laughable to think of them spending multiple hours randomly surfing the Web during the school day. But clearly, the temptation is there, and it will only be heightened as more of our lives drift into the cloud and the devices we use get steadily smarter. We all have things that need to be done online and rarely do we have enough time to get them all done. Smart school districts, like other savvy employers, will develop acceptable use policies that have a little bit of flexibility, to give people the option to spend personal time on the Web during lunch or after students have left. That can go a long way towards reducing the temptation to click on "just one more site" while students are supposedly reading or taking a test.

But a cautionary word: Regardless of the precise terms of a district's acceptable use policy, never forget that everything done online using the school network can be recorded and can easily be reviewed by administrators. The district IT department may also have deployed alerts to flag visits to inappropriate Web sites, which will inevitably spark further investigation. Cyberloafing is a cybertrap that is particularly easy to document, in the unfortunate instance of complaints about teacher performance, or worse, student endangerment.

~~~~~~~~~

Chapter Two
Hostile Work Environments

No one could seriously argue that hostile work environments are merely an unfortunate byproduct of the Internet era. Just watch a few episodes of "Mad Men" to get a rough idea of how actively unpleasant or casually oppressive office environments could be for women and minority groups in the 1950s, 60s, 70s—well, pick pretty much any decade. And undoubtedly, the actual day-to-day experience was much worse than the glossy and relatively sanitized 30 or 60-minute versions that are served up for television audience.

But as with so many other aspects of contemporary life, electronic devices (computers, smartphones, tablets) and the programs they run make it much easier and far faster for employees (including teachers) to generate or propagate a hostile environment.

A hostile work environment is created when an employer or a co-worker repeatedly acts towards someone in such a way as to make it impossible for the targeted individual to do his or her job. Generally speaking under United States law, a single off-color joke or offensive remark is not sufficient to create a hostile work environment. Instead, an employee must be able to show that he or she has been subjected to conduct that rises to the level of **harassment**.

The National Education Association, the largest teacher union in the United States, offers its affiliates and school districts model contract language, in which "harassment" is defined as follows:

> Harassment/intimidation exists if an individual or group: directs personal insults (whether transmitted in writing, orally, or by electronic means) that are likely to incite an immediate adverse response from the person(s) being addressed; threatens the employee with physical harm or actually harms a person; damages, defaces or destroys private property of any person; commits an act of harassment or intimidation (as defined by statute); [or] places a person in position of feeling at risk of emotional or psychological harm.[2.1]

A particularly good example of the powerful role of electronics in modern-day hostile workplace cases occurred a few years ago in the Chippewa Falls School District. In January 2010, a fellow teacher filed a workplace harassment complaint against fifth-grade teacher Elizabeth McElhenny, alleging that McElhenny had "target[ed] students, staff, and administration in an ongoing aggressive and belligerent effort to control and undermine the operations of Hillcrest Elementary School that spans back several years[.]"[2.2]

The district promptly launched an investigation into McElhenny's conduct during the preceding year, and issued a report of its findings at the end of August, 2010. Among other things, the report concluded that the amount of time that

McElhenny spent using the District email system was "excessive and inappropriate." Investigators concluded that over the course of 169 class days from January 2009 to January 2010, McElhenny sent 3,811 emails, or an average of 23 per day. Based on the time-stamp associated with each email, the District was able to determine that McElhenny spent a total of 38 hours of class time and 19 hours of prep time using email (based on a highly conservative estimate of 1 minute per email).

But while the amount of time McElhenny spent emailing was obviously a productivity concern, the real issue was what she was writing to fellow teachers. In a summary article for *The Chippewa Herald*, reporter Liz Hochstedler cited numerous examples of McElhenny's inappropriate messages:

- She alluded to alcohol as "water," and often said that she "had too much 'water' last night."
- She used the abbreviations "praz" and "vico" to refer to the prescription drugs Alprazolam and Vicodin, and wrote about her usage frequently. In one typical example, McElhenny wrote: "i could tell my 4:30t this morning that it was going to be THAT KIND OF DAY 1/2 praz every 3 hours started at 7:10 this morning and will continue taking a nibble of my magic relaxing potion every 3 hours."
- She used a long list of epithets for co-workers, including: "cult members," "nutjob," "crabbypants," "cuckoo woman" and "Nazi aides."

- She regaled her co-workers with descriptions of various sexual encounters.

- She frequently referred to students and parents in demeaning ways. For example, she wrote in one email: "could that student possibly be [student initials removed]? I am very familiar with that THING and also with his mother THING 2 He is the first person that comes to mind... ... Do not allow him to SUCK THE LIFE OUT OF YOU!"[2,3]

McElhenny apparently had some latent understanding that her email correspondence might be a problem, since she worried about the risk of using school email for inappropriate conversations and frequently asked colleagues to destroy the emails she sent. However, she didn't have a great grasp of computer forensics or the durability of digital information. Given the fact that school districts are required to maintain staff communications in most states pursuant to public records laws, it's not surprising that District investigators had little trouble recreating McElhenny's exhaustive and somewhat scandalous email correspondence.

Shortly before the investigatory report was released, McElhenny resigned from the Chippewa Falls School District. At the same time, she filed a lawsuit seeking an injunction against the release of the report, but withdrew the lawsuit the following day.[24] A few months later, McElhenny announced her candidacy for a position on the Chippewa Falls School Board, but dropped out of the race shortly before the April 2011 election. Fittingly, she announced her withdrawal in an email to supporters and the media.

"This past year or so has been very difficult for me and hard on my family," McElhenny said in her statement. "Personal aspects of my private and professional life have been made public in some media condemning me for being human." She said that her goal was to get her life "back to normal", and added that "I will not be able to do that if I run for the school board and am elected, especially if I will have to butt philosophical heads with people who have little understanding of the complexity of issues that are truly important to running a school district effectively."[2.5]

McElhenny's case is just one example of how easily electronic media can be used to create a hostile work environment. In fact, there is growing concern in education circles about the phenomenon of teacher-on-teacher bullying and cyberbullying. Just as with kids, the increase in the number of mobile devices used by educators parallels this rise in not-so-collegial behavior. The perception of anonymity (however flawed) and the ability to harass someone without physical confrontation help lure adults into many of the same cybertraps that snare children.

Another common aspect of this cybertrap lies in the fact that sometimes, a hostile work environment can be created without direct communication between educators. Prior to the arrival of the Internet, the most typical example would be the shop teacher or football coach who taped Playboy centerfolds to the walls of his office. Now, like any other employer that relies on computers and Internet access to function, school districts need to be concerned about the very real possibility that educators, staff, and/or administrators are using school computers or their own mobile devices to look at pornography on school grounds. Employers of every description awoke to the issue of porn in the workplace in the late 1990s and early 2000s. The growing popularity of adult web sites, combined with the fact that employers typically had faster Internet connections than workers, meant that many people spent time (often hours each day) visiting porn sites.[26]

In response, employers began implementing increasingly powerful software to monitor employee Web surfing habits, but a decade later, it's not clear how effective computer surveillance has been in preventing on-the-job porn surfing. In September 2013, for instance, a survey done in the United Kingdom of nearly 4,000 businesses by the employment law firm Peninsula Business Services found that two-thirds of the companies had caught someone looking at porn on the job during the previous year. That was double the rate in 2008.[27] Studies that rely on self-reporting suggest that somewhere between three percent[28] and twenty-eight percent[29] of American workers access pornography at work.

If a school employee's preferred form of cyberloafing does in fact involve visiting adult Web sites, a district may find itself facing a hostile work environment claim from other employees who are offended by the practice. Of course, the viewing of pornography on school property raises a number of other significant concerns, including: damage to co-worker morale; desensitization to sexual harassment; embarrassment for the school district; and possible damage to the district's computers from malware."[2.10] And of course, school districts face one serious issue the average employer does not: the possible exposure of young children to sexually explicit materials.

Educators who actively and frequently seek out adult materials during school hours, particularly when students are around, are clearly behaving badly and risking their careers. Most of the time, the behavior is so egregious and so blatant that there's really no question that discipline should be imposed. A few quick examples underscore the global nature of this problem:

- A teacher at a German private school in Bonn was suspended and put under investigation in November 2013 after students "credibly" reported that the teacher repeatedly watched pornography instead of giving instruction in science.[2.11]

- A teacher at the Reynella East College, a K-12 school in Adelaide, Australia was recently suspended with full pay while the Teachers Registration Board of South Australia investigates charges that he used a student's ID to visit adult Web sites featuring violent pornography. (The student, who spent the better part of a year being accused of the activity, was ultimately paid $30,000 AUD in exchange for a confidentiality agreement that protected the teacher and the school.)[2.12]

- A teacher in New Zealand was censured and given a two-year suspension after losing a personal USB device during a school picnic day on school property. The device was found by school officials and an examination revealed pornographic materials. A review of the teacher's school-issued laptop showed that he had used it to access pornography Web sites (although not on school grounds). The discipline was imposed due to the risk of exposure of harmful materials by students (who might have found the USB device) and violation of the school's acceptable use policy.[2.13]

Unfortunately, online pornography is so pervasive and electronically insidious that even educators with little or no interest in adult materials are at risk of this particular cybertrap. Under the wrong circumstances, a single careless click can destroy an entire career.

That's basically what happened in 2004 to Julie Amero, then a 37-year-old substitute teacher at the Kelly Middle School in Norwich, Connecticut. One morning, she used her classroom computer to check her personal email, and then went to the bathroom. When she came back, Amero saw two students standing in front of the computer, laughing, as a rapid series of sexually explicit images were displayed. Amero desperately tried to close the images, but each click caused more pop-ups to appear (a form of "mousetrapping" commonly referred to in the adult industry as a "circle jerk"). Over the next several hours, she continued her efforts to clean up the screen, but eventually had to get help from the school's vice principal.[2.14]

In a predictable sequence of events, Amero's students told their parents what had happened, middle school administrators began to get angry complaints, and the principal notified the local police about the incident. A few days later, Amero was arrested and charged with ten counts of "risk of injury to a minor," on the theory that she was surfing pornography sites in the classroom. Among other things, prosecutors argued that if Amero were innocent, she would have simply turned off the computer; Amero, however, testified that the computer was a new resource and that she had never been taught how to do that. The State of Connecticut eventually dropped six of the charges, but that still left Amero facing a possible **40 years** in state prison. Prosecutors offered Amero a plea agreement that would have cleared her record in two years with good behavior, but she rejected it, saying that she was the innocent victim of a computer virus.[2.15]

Amero was convicted of all four counts on January 5, 2007, but reports of the weak and flawed computer forensics evidence offered at trial caused an uproar among computer security specialists around the country. With the help of some *pro bono* forensics analysis (and a re-examination of the computer's hard drive by the state lab), Amero's attorney was able to get the original verdict set aside.[2.16] A year and a half later, prosecutors agreed to drop the felony charges altogether and allow Amero to plead guilty to a misdemeanor for "disorderly conduct". She paid a $100 file, but more significantly, lost her Connecticut teaching credentials.[2.17]

There is a wide-spread consensus that Amero's prosecution was, from the very outset, a perfect storm of administrative overreaction, prosecutorial zeal, political posturing, and forensic incompetence. This precise type of case is unlikely to occur in the future, as computer forensics tools and techniques are becoming increasingly sophisticated. While that might be good news for teachers like Amero who are assaulted by viral activity, it's less good news for teachers whose porn-surfing is more extensive than they originally are willing to admit.

In 2006, for instance, Robert Zellner, a biology teacher and union leader in Cedarburg, WI, disabled the Google Safe Search setting on his school computer and spent a grand total of 67 seconds viewing the search results for the word "blonde." Not surprisingly, many of the search results were pornographic, but as his browser history clearly demonstrated, Zellner did not visit any of the links provided by Google. (He later argued that he was concerned about students accessing adult materials on school computers and wanted to test the district's filtering software.[2.18])

Zellner had signed the school's acceptable use policy, which prohibited such activity, but he may not have been aware that the school's IT department had installed monitoring software on his computer (and his alone, it later turned out). A report of Zellner's Google Search activity was given to Cedarburg Superintendent Daryl Herrick, along with allegations that Zellner had surfed pornography on prior occasions, and had kept photos of bikini-clad students taken during a school trip to Hawaii. Herrick told Zellner either to resign or face public disclosure and dismissal. Zellner refused, and was forced to endure an unusual public hearing on his conduct before the Cedarburg School Board, which subsequently fired him.[2.19]

After various court proceedings at the state level (all of which ended in favor of the school district), Zellner filed a $9 million federal lawsuit in 2008, alleging that he was not fired because of inappropriate Internet activity, but instead in retaliation for his union activities (which, if true, would be a violation of Zellner's First Amendment rights). The U.S. District Court granted summary judgment in favor the School District, and that decision was affirmed by the U.S. Court of Appeals for the 7th Circuit on April 29, 2011, which wrote:

> [Zellner] directly and knowingly violated a School Board Policy. He admitted as much in front of the Board at his hearing and apologized for his actions. Zellner thus failed to establish proof that the Google Image search was a pretext for firing him. Without evidence that some other teacher violated the Policy in a similar way and received a milder sanction, Zellner's

"but for" case rests on conjecture. Accordingly, he cannot rebut the District's legitimate, non-discriminatory reason for his termination. The judge correctly granted the District's motion for summary judgment with respect to Zellner's First Amendment claim."

Among the lessons to be learned from the Zellner case (in addition to the fact that even the briefest stroll on the dark side of the Web can be a problem) is that computers now give school districts the ability to reach far into the past to harvest evidence of possible misconduct.

~~~~~~~~~

Chapter Three
Illegal Online Activity

With a few short key strokes, the network we now know as the Internet sprang into being on October 29, 1969. Originally called "ARPANET" (the acronym stood for Advanced Research Projects Agency Network), the infant network was a research initiative of interest only to scientists and academics; what we think of as the Internet today, a commercially vibrant communication tool linking people around the globe, did not begin to emerge until the late 1980s. It exploded into public consciousness in 1993 and 1994, when the release of the first graphical Web browser, Mosaic, made it possible to easily view text, images, and even video on the same screen.

In those early days of the Internet, very few people gave much thought to the possibility that the emerging network could be used for criminal purposes. To be fair, it didn't take long for annoyances to arise: the first spam, for instance, was sent over the ARPANET on May 3, 1978 by Gary Thuerk, a marketer for the now-defunct Digital Equipment Corporation.[3.1] And just four years later, when Apple still held its short-lived lead as the dominant personal computer brand, a fourteen-year-old named Rich Skrenta created the first virus, a boot-sector infection called "Elk Cloner."[3.2] Despite its significant place in computing history, however, Skrenta's virus was fairly harmless; every fiftieth time that an infected disk was used to start an Apple II personal computer, the virus would first display a poem written by Skrenta.[3.3]

In the thirty years since Skrenta's little joke, however, cybercrime has become a multi-billion dollar business and a massive global problem. A July 2013 study by the software security firm McAfee estimated that the worldwide cost of cybercrime and cyberespionage could be as high as**$400 billion** per year. Admittedly, that's just a tiny slice of the planet's $70 trillion of gross domestic product (GDP), but still, $400 billion is real money.[3.4]

The range of criminal activities that occur online is discouragingly impressive. A small but representative list of electronic crimes includes: virus and malware distribution, hacking, cyber theft, software piracy, copyright infringement, fraud, cyberharassment and cyberstalking, phishing and Trojan attacks, identity theft, voyeurism, sexting, and so on. And of course, new and disturbingly creative criminal activities pop up with remarkable frequency.

Crime statistics, cyber or otherwise, are unfortunately not broken down by the profession of the person who committed the crime, so there is no easy way to tell if educators are more or less likely to commit some types of cybercrimes as compared to other professionals. After more than a decade of researching online activity, however, I can say anecdotally that educators do not commit cybercrimes more frequently than other types of professionals; in fact, the overall percentage of electronic misbehavior by teachers is probably lower than among other types of workers.

That being said, a small percentage of educators unquestionably do commit online crimes, which run the gamut of possible offenses. As the following cases illustrate, teachers can all too easily find themselves ensnared in a variety of different criminal cybertraps. The motivations for these crimes by teachers, needless to say, are no different from the impulses that spur criminal behavior in any other segment of the population: greed, desperation, jealousy, anger, bitterness, sociopathy, bad judgment, even mere boredom.

In some instances, a good argument can be made that a teacher's criminal behavior stems from the same immature social impulses that all too often motivate their students. For instance, in 2008, Richard Naylor, a computer and accounting teacher at North Warren Regional High School in Pennsylvania, was apparently angry over treatment he received from a couple of male students. Following the dispute (the exact nature of which was unspecified), Naylor sent multiple threatening emails to the two male students, despite being asked by fellow teachers and parents to stop. He also hacked into the AOL account of one of the boys and sent a message to the boy's girlfriend, announcing that the two were breaking up. Naylor ultimately pleaded guilty to stalking and harassing the three students. He was ordered to forfeit his teaching license and spend five years on probation with a variety of conditions, including psychiatric evaluation.[3.5]

More typically, however, an educator's computer misconduct is driven by self-interest, or a desire to protect colleagues or the school district. In 2012, a drunk 16-year-old girl was assaulted at multiple parties in Steubenville, Ohio; her assailants, mostly members of the high school football team, took photos and videos of the girl during the attacks and posted them to various social media sites, including Facebook, Twitter, and Instagram. In May 2013, two members of the football team were convicted of rape. Five months after their trial, several school district employees were indicted on a variety of charges related to the incident. Two of the employees, District Superintendent Mike McVey and IT director William Rhinaman, were charged with assorted computer-related crimes, including the erasure of "evidence that included emails and data on computer hard drives." Investigators alleged that McVey instructed Rhinaman to carry out the deletions. McVey is scheduled to go to trial on the charges in January 2015; if convicted, he faces up to five years in prison. No trial date has been set yet for Rhinaman.[3.6]

One of the more interesting and convoluted cybertraps involving a teacher occurred during the 2014 mid-term elections. Over the summer, a particularly nasty Republican primary battle was raging in Mississippi between long-time incumbent Thad Cochran and his Tea Party-supported challenger, Chris McDaniel. In mid-May, a local blogger named Chris Kelly was arrested after posting a surreptitious video of Cochran's wife Rose at the St. Catherine's Village nursing facility, where she has lived for more than 14 years. A short time later, police arrested several other individuals for allegedly conspiring with Kelly to obtain and publish the video. In addition to conspiracy, prosecutors charged Richard Sager, a physical education teacher at Laurel High School in Laurel, Mississippi, with tampering with electronic evidence. Sager, who faces up to five years in prison for conspiracy and two years for the tampering, is actively engaged in plea negotiations.[3.7]

While not technically a "cybertrap," it's worth noting that for some teachers, computers are not so much the instruments of a crime as the crime itself. In the fall of 2013, the Rhinelander (WI) Board of Education unanimously terminated the contract of high school English teacher Joshua Juergens after he was charged with stealing over $9,000 of school computer equipment. Juergens was also charged with raising marijuana in his home, and was under investigation for other possible computer thefts.[3.8]

If human history tells us anything, it's that crime will happen, and I am certainly realistic enough to know that nothing in this book is going to change that. Inevitably, some percentage of teachers will use electronic devices and online services to commit criminal acts. However, the incidence of criminal activity can be significantly reduced through an emphasis on ethical guidelines and conduct, professional development, and appropriate district supervision.

~~~~~~~~~

Chapter Four
The Hidden Cybertrap: Mishandling of Student Sexts

By now, most people have heard of the narcissistic photo known as the "selfie," the practice of using a camera and mirror, or simply an outstretched smartphone, to take a photo of oneself. The practice has become so ubiquitous, in fact, that "selfie" was designated 2013's "Word of the Year" by the Oxford University Press.[4.1]

Selfies come in a vast array of categories, from the quizzical "How do this outfit look on me?" to the memorial "Shameless Selfie at Machu Picchu" [courtesy of TripAdvisor.com] to the self-congratulatory Hillary Clinton and Meryl Streep at 2012 Kennedy Center Honors to the wildly inappropriate "Selfies at Funerals."

A related phenomenon emerged in the mid-2000s, as cellphones grew steadily more sophisticated. In a 2004 article covering an alleged affair between soccer star David Beckham and his assistant Rebecca Loos, *The Globe and Mail* reporter Josey Vogels was apparently the first to refer to the practice of sending salacious text messages as "sext messaging."[4.2] By late 2008/early 2009, the word "sext" was firmly established as a shorthand for sexually explicit text messages or images being sent from one cellphone to another.

2004 happened to be the same year that cellphone manufactures began concentrating on teens as a previously untapped market. At the time, just about 25% of teens used a cellphone. By 2008, that percentage would double and then nearly double again over the next four years. Today, just under 95% of high school students have a cellphone and the majority of those are smartphones. The devices allow students to take increasingly high-resolution photos and videos and instantaneously share them with their friends, classmates, and the world.

A confluence of powerful social trends—computers, the Internet, the initial success of the online adult industry, easy access to pornography, the rise of "porn chic," and the ready availability of cellphones—made it inevitable that children would start sexting.[43] By 2009, the National Campaign to Prevent Teen and Unplanned Pregnancy was reporting that 20% of teens were taking, sending, and redistributing naked photos of themselves or other children.[44]

It didn't take long for sexting to become a problem for educators and school districts, one that has often had tragic consequences. One of the earliest examples—a story that helped inspire *Cybertraps for the Young*—occurred in Cincinnati, Ohio in 2008. A young woman named Jessica Logan, 18, sent nude pictures of herself to her boyfriend. When they stopped going out, the boyfriend forwarded the photos to friends of his, who then forwarded them to others. During the ensuing investigation, one area school board member later told me, copies of Logan's photographs were found in seven different high schools in the Cincinnati area.

As the photos spread, Logan suffered terrible abuse: other students harassed her both physically and verbally (typical epithets included "slut" and "whore"). Logan, formerly a popular and successful student, began skipping class and showing other signs of depression. In an effort to protect other girls, Logan made an appearance on a local Cincinnati television station (with blurred image and altered voice) to warn of the dangers of sexting. Her mother, Cynthia Logan, said that she seemed to be doing better after graduation in May, but tragically, Jessica Logan hanged herself in her bedroom in July 2008.[4.5] Around the United States, and around the world, there have been dozens of other instances in which post-sexting bullying has played a role (often significant) in the suicide deaths of teens and even pre-teens.

The Logan case vividly illustrates why school districts should take student sexting cases seriously. Some districts have tried to fall back on the defense that the sexting did not occur on school grounds—in fact, that's precisely the reason given by the superintendent of Sycamore Schools, where Logan was a student, as to why her tormentors were not punished.[4.6] However, there is an emerging legal consensus that school districts should intervene even in situations that occur off-campus or purely online, where the behavior has "a direct and immediate effect on either school safety or the safety and welfare of students and staff."[4.7] Not surprisingly, some of that legal consensus is being driven by litigation, as families like the Logans seek to recover damages from school districts and individual administrators for not doing enough to protect their children from bullying.

Teachers and administrators run relatively little risk when investigating allegations of purely text-based cyberharassment or cyberbullying. The primary concerns are the efficacy of the investigations, respecting student privacy to the extent possible, and following established procedures to ensure due process. But when the investigation centers around the production and distribution of sexting images of minors, teachers and administrators need to be very cautious in how they proceed. With all the daily pressures educators face, including demanding parents and inadequate supervisory guidelines, what seem like routine decisions can have dramatic consequences. Couple this complex and hectic profession with a determined and unsympathetic prosecutor, and educators might find themselves facing life-altering child pornography charges.

The leading object lesson of how that can happen involves Ting-Yi Oei, an assistant principal at Freedom High School in South Riding, Virginia. In the spring of 2008, a teacher alerted Oei of a rumor making the rounds of the high school that students were sending nude photos to each other, and Oei was asked to investigate what was happening.

Oei did not know the identity of any students involved in the alleged incident, but he thought he knew the name of a student who might know something about it. Oei called the student into the office and in the presence of the school's safety and security specialist, asked him about the rumor. The student admitted that he had received a nude photo and showed it to the school officials; according to Oei's account, the image showed the torso of a female, dressed in panties and arms crossed over her breasts. Oei took the student's cellphone to school principal Christine Forester, showed her the photo, and was told to keep a copy of the photo on his computer for safekeeping in case it was needed later in the investigation.[4.8]

Although Oei had been given poorly instructed, everything was still fine at that point. But Oei did not know how to get the photo from the student's cellphone to his computer, and the school's IT department couldn't help.[4.9] Undoubtedly seeing an opportunity to be cooperative, the student volunteered to text the photo to Oei's phone, and then helped Oei email the photo from Oei's cellphone to his school computer. According to Oei, all of this transpired in front of the Freedom High School safety and security specialist.[4.10]

Oei continued his investigation by interviewing other students (including, it later turned out, the girl who was the subject of the photo), but no one volunteered any additional information. Oei told the principal that there was no way to identify the girl in the photo, and the matter was dropped. Since no disciplinary action was being taken against the male student who showed Oei the photo, Oei saw no reason to notify his parents.[4.11] It was also a particularly stressful time for Oei, whose wife was facing surgery for a potentially fatal tumor, and Oei was scheduled to meet with her physician as soon as he could leave school that afternoon.

The very morning Oei returned from leave following his wife's surgery, he was forced to bring the young man who provided the sexting photo into his office again, this time for engaging in a practice called "flagging," which the *Urban Dictionary* defines as "the act of pulling another person's pants down."[4.12] Oei called the boy's mother to tell her that the student would be suspended and advised her that the victim could pursue an assault charge. During the course of the conversation, Oei mentioned the earlier incident. As Oei himself later said, "She was outraged that I hadn't reported it to her at the time." She was also angry that her son was being suspended, and after her appeal was rejected by the principal, threatened Oei with legal action.[4.13]

A few days later, two investigators from the Loudon County Sheriff's office visited Oei and asked to see the photo he had received from the male student. The investigators told Oei they were responding to a parental complaint, which turned out to an act of retaliation by the mother of the male student. Oei was unable to locate the photo on his computer, but remembered that a copy was on his cellphone. He turned his cellphone over to the investigators, who examined the photo and then returned the cellphone to Oei. There was, according to Oei, no suggestion that he himself was under investigation for any reason.

It came as quite a shock, then, when the Commonwealth's Attorney for Loudon County, Jim Plowman, announced that

Oei was being charged with "failure to report suspected child abuse." The charges were eventually dropped in the early summer of 2008, in part because it was not clear under Virginia law how consensual behavior (in this case, the taking of a photo) between two minors could be construed as "abuse," and even it could, Oei had complied with Virginia's law by reporting the photo to the school's principal. But Plowman, whose campaign for Commonwealth's Attorney had been based on a promise of much stricter law enforcement, told Oei that if he did not resign from his job, he would face a felony charge for possession of child pornography. Deputy Commonwealth's Attorney Nicole Wittmann told reporters that "We just feel very strongly that this is not someone who should be in the Loudoun County school system."[4.14]

Oei refused to resign, believing that he had acted properly during his investigation and that the image on his phone did not even constitute child pornography. But as Oei told Michel Martin on National Public Radio, "I think there are other issues, too, of perhaps the prosecutor thinking that this is indeed something that his name and reputation are tied to, and this is his way of going about—to showing it."[4.15] Regardless of Plowman's precise motive—political or legal—Oei was indicted on August 11, 2008 on one count of possession of child pornography, a charge that carried a possible sentence of five years. Four months later, Plowman's office added two additional misdemeanor counts for "contributing to the delinquency of a minor," each of which could have added an additional year to Oei's ultimate sentence. The objective, clearly, was to put more pressure on Oei to resign his position and accept a guilty plea.

In March 2009, Oei's attorney Steven Stone filed a motion to dismiss all of the charges on the grounds that the image in question did not constitute child pornography, and the motion was granted a month later by Loudoun Circuit Court Judge Thomas Horne. The judge ruled that in order for an image to constitute "child pornography" under Virginia law, it must be "sexually explicit" and "lewd." Mere nudity, he said, is not sufficient.[4.16]

Following the court's decision, Plowman (who is still serving as the Commonwealth's Attorney for Loudon County) said that the case would never have gotten so far along if Oei had simply resigned when "asked" to do so. "I thought that was a just and appropriate sanction for his behavior," Plowman told *Wired*'s Kim Zetter. "But he was unwilling to be responsible for any kind of accountability for what he did."

The ordeal left Oei with uncertain job prospects and massive legal fees, but the story had a (quasi-)happy ending. A month after the criminal charges were dismissed, the Loudon County School Board voted 7-1 to reimburse him $168,000, and he received a warm welcome from colleagues and staff when he returned to his position as assistant principal at Freedom High School. But not surprisingly, the experience left him wounded and upset.

"And so my legal ordeal is done," he wrote in the *Washington Post*, "but I still ask myself: Did anyone benefit from all this? I have to put the pieces of my life and career back together. My wife and I were terrorized by a baseless prosecution, lost all our savings and were forced to borrow huge sums of money to pay for my defense. The students involved probably could have put this ill-advised sexting adventure behind them a long time ago. Instead, they had to wonder for months whether they'd have to testify in court and bring attention to themselves and their families. And a meaningful discussion about sexting and what schools, parents, the community and law enforcement can do about it has been sidetracked for more than a year by a prosecutor who should never have brought charges in the first place."[4.17]

Oei's summary echoes the plaintive question of former United States Labor Secretary Ray Donovan, who was charged in 1987 with grand larceny and fraud in connection with a construction project in New York. After being acquitted of all charges, he famously asked, "Which office do I go to get my reputation back?" But Donovan had the relative benefit of experiencing his travails before the World Wide Web came along to digitally tattoo each of us with our successes and failures; the prosecution against him has largely faded into historical obscurity. Oei's experience may be an extreme example of the toxic mix of prosecutorial zeal, self-righteous parenting, and technological ignorance, but the cold reality is that as a result of a small misstep, any educator could find himself or herself stamped forever online with the label of "child pornographer." Every educator should insist that their district adopt clear and well-vetted procedures for handling potentially sensitive material during in-school investigations.

~~~~~~~~~

Chapter Five
Receipt and Possession of Child Pornography

Not surprisingly, the category of online criminal activity that attracts the most attention and concern is anything having to do with child pornography. Wholly apart from a teacher's overall position as a role model in society, the fact that teachers work with children for hours each day makes any involvement with child pornography deeply disturbing.[5.1]

"Child pornography" is defined under federal law as "any visual depiction, including any photograph, film, video, picture, or computer or computer-generated image or picture, whether made or produced by electronic, mechanical, or other means, of sexually explicit conduct, where the production of such visual depiction involves the use of a minor engaging in sexually explicit conduct..."[5.2] A "minor," is defined as someone under the age of 18, which covers the majority of students in a K-12 school system.[5.3]

Unfortunately, one of the darker side effects of the Internet has been the resurgence in the production and distribution of child pornography. I clerked for a U.S. District Court in Massachusetts from 1988 to 1990, and worked on a couple of federal child pornography prosecutions. The evidence in the cases was generated through undercover work by the U.S. Postal Service, which over the years had developed highly effective techniques for identifying possible child pornography consumers and collecting evidence against them.

With the online world still in its infancy, the vast majority of child pornography transactions involved magazines or videotapes, which had to be shipped from one location to another. When the Postal Service or the FBI raided distributors of child pornography, they would often operate the businesses for a period of time and solicit orders from people looking for contraband material. Before sending out the requested material, the FBI would obtain a search warrant for the customer's home, and then coordinate delivery with the Postal Service. Fifteen to twenty minutes after delivery, the FBI would execute the search warrant, and nine times out of ten, find the video playing on the TV or the magazine open on the coffee table. The precise timing was important, since it helped eliminate any claim by the defendant that he did not know the nature of material that had been delivered. The investigative collaboration among the Postal Service, the FBI, and other federal agencies was so effective that the general consensus in the late 1980s was that commercial production and spread of child pornography had all but been stopped.

No one claimed that the scourge of child pornography had been entirely eliminated, but certainly, its production and distribution was far riskier than it had been in the past. But then, in rapid-fire succession, came a series of technological innovations that completely reversed those law enforcement gains. By the late 1980s, of course, the Internet had been around for twenty years and the personal computer for ten, but their use was largely limited to the creation and transmission of text in one form or another. But even so, enterprising child pornographers were already beginning to explore the possible uses of these new technologies.

In 1980, for instance, a 38-year-old electrical engineer named John Likins was charged with selling and conspiracy to distribute child pornography. When law enforcement searched Likins's home, they found over 2,500 feet of computer printouts listing various types of child pornography available from around the United States, as well as the names of hundreds of potential customers. Investigators said that they believed Likins was planning to use his Heath "microcomputer" to launch the first (and at the time, the only) "computerized child pornography in the world."[5.4]

Over the next several years, an increasing number of reports emerged that child pornographers were using home computers to catalog their collections of contraband,[5.5] maintain diaries and journals of their sexual assaults,[5.6] and eventually, communicate directly with other collectors and producers of child pornography on computer bulletin boards.[5.7]

Three new technologies, however, were emerging that would dramatically exacerbate the child pornography problem. The first was the personal scanner, which allowed consumers to scan pictures (like old *Playboy* magazines) and share them online. As with all technology, these devices were hideously expensive at first, but then rapidly got much cheaper. In 1987, for instance, a gray-scale desktop scanner cost somewhere between \$3,000 and \$10,000[5.8]; by 1992, the cost of a **color** scanner had fallen to less than \$1,500.[5.9]

The second was the digital camera. In 1986, Kodak developed the first megapixel imaging chip, which made it possible to create a good-quality 5x7 inch print from a digital image. It took somewhat longer for that technology to become widely adopted, in part because prices remained staggeringly high for years. In 1994, for instance, even a low-end digital camera still cost about \$1,000, and magazines were casually reviewing models that cost eleven times as much.[5.10]

The third technology was the World Wide Web, an idea that had been percolating in the mind of Timothy Berners-Lee, a researcher at the CERN facility in Switzerland, since 1980. In March 1989, he wrote up a proposal for "a large hypertext database with typed links." With encouragement from his boss Mike Sendall and assistance from fellow research Robert Cailliau, Berners-Lee constructed the basic elements of the World Wide Web operating on CERN computers by December 1990. The following month, non-CERN web servers connected to Berners-Lee's network for the first time, and the World Wide Web was off and running.

Taken together, these three technologies—scanners, digital cameras, and the World Wide Web—fueled a tragic explosion in the production and distribution of child pornography around the globe. Scanners have given new life to old print images (thus perpetuating acts of abuse that took place decades ago), digital cameras have made it easy to produce new images without running the risk of film developers reporting questionable images to the police, and the World Wide Web has facilitated both nearly-instantaneous global distribution of contraband images and the development of far-flung underground communities devoted to the sharing and sale of these images. Over the past two decades, child pornography has exploded into a global problem and a significant priority for law enforcement agencies around the world.

Like people from every other walk of life, teachers have found it all too easy to fall into this particularly nasty cybertrap. Not a single week goes by without multiple reports of teachers being arrested, indicted, and convicted for receiving, distributing, and producing child pornography. The stories are a living journal of the constantly-evolving cat-and-mouse game between perpetrators and police. Teachers have been caught using peer-to-peer software, offering to trade child pornography in chat rooms, setting up meetings in classrooms to exchange child pornography on USB sticks, taking surreptitious photos of students on field trips, soliciting and receiving sexting photos from underage students—the catalog of methodologies is virtually endless.

It is important to reiterate again and again that these types of cases, while horrifying, are fortunately exceedingly rare. The actual number of educators involved in child pornography is a tiny percentage of the roughly 3 million K-12 teachers employed in the United States. Nonetheless, even a single victim is one too many, and we need to use every possible tool—pre-certification training, an ethical code for educators, effective background checks, professional development, and ongoing supervision—to better protect not only students but any child who is victimized by child pornography.

~~~~~~~~~

Section II
Cybertraps Outside of the Workplace

1905 Teaching Contract for Story County, Iowa

1. Teachers are expected to live in the community in which they are employed and to take residence with local citizens for room and board.

2. Teachers will be required to spend weekends in the community unless permission is granted by the Chairman of the Board.

3. It is understood that teachers will attend church each Sunday and take an active part, particularly in choir and Sunday School work.

4. Dancing, card playing and the theatre are works of the Devil that lead to gambling, immoral climate, and influence and will not be tolerated.

5. Community plays are given annually. Teachers are expected to participate.

6. When laundering petticoats and unmentionables it is best to dry them in a flour sack or pillow case.

7. Any teacher who smokes cigarettes, uses liquor in any form, frequents a pool or public hall, or gets shaved in a barber shop, bobbs [*sic*] her hair, has dyed hair, wears short skirts and has undue use of cosmetics will not be tolerated under any circumstances.

8. Teachers will not marry or keep company with a man friend during the week except as an escort to church

services.

9. Loitering in ice cream parlors, drug stores, etc., is prohibited.

10. Purchasing or reading the Sunday Supplement on the Sabbath will not be tolerated.

11. Discussing political views or party choice is not advisable.

12. Men teachers may take one evening each week for courting purposes or two evenings a week if they go to church regularly.

13. After 10 hours in school, the teacher should spend the remaining time reading the Bible or other good books.

14. Women teachers who marry or engage in other unseemly conduct will be dismissed.

15. Every teacher should lay aside from his pay a goodly sum for his declining years so that he will not become a burden on society.

16. The teacher who performs his labors faithfully and without fault for five years will be given an increase of 25 cents a week in his pay providing the Board of Education approves.[61]

~~~~~~~~~~

Chapter Six
Are Educators Entitled to a Personal Life?

The title of this chapter is not an entirely facetious question. Educators may have the lowest inherent expectation of privacy of any professionals in American society. Much of that has to do with the fact that educators are expected to fill dual roles in the classroom, as both content providers and moral role models to their students. As a result, the actions of teachers both in and out of the classroom are closely scrutinized by district administrators, school boards, parents, and increasingly, the media (a term which now for all practical purposes applies to anyone with a smartphone).

This is a long-standing tradition. From the start of the American public school system, local school boards placed as much if not more emphasis on a teacher's moral character as on his or her ability to teach. In part, this was to set a good example for the students, but community leaders also wanted to be sure that their teachers were focusing on their work and not on frivolous activities. As a local history guide to the Harn Homestead in Oklahoma put it, "School boards expected teachers to focus all their attention on teaching duties; strict standards of behavior were required from all teachers."[6.2]

Not surprisingly, given the social conventions of the 19th century, female teachers were subjected to the closest scrutiny regarding the morality of their behavior. "While teaching was a respectable profession for young women," the Harn Homestead guide said, "they could not marry; it was considered unseemly and distracting from their duties. If the teacher was a local woman, she could live at home with her family; otherwise, she was expected to board with the families of her students. Generally this meant that the teacher shared a room with the children and had no privacy at all."[6.3]

School board interest in the romantic lives of teachers intensified during the Great Depression. With jobs increasingly scarce, school boards reached the dubious conclusion that married female teachers did not need to work, since they could be supported by their husbands. By 1928, according to a survey conducted at the time by the National Education Association, nearly thirty percent of school districts with populations over 2,500 had adopted regulations that required a woman to resign as soon as she got married.[6.4]

As was the case with so many other categories of employment, World War II dramatically changed hiring practices in the teaching profession. The vacancies created throughout the U.S. economy by military mobilization offered single women unprecedented job opportunities, and they left teaching in droves. Faced with a rapidly growing shortage of teachers, districts were forced to drop their prohibitions against married teachers. The baby boom that ensued when the soldiers came home kept the demand for teachers high, and for the most part, the marriage bars faded into history. In fact, for a variety of reasons—including growing suspicion of and prejudice against "spinsters"—by

1960, the percentage of married teachers was twice that of single women.[6.5]

One restriction that lingered long after the prohibitions against married teachers disappeared was the ban on visibly pregnant women in the classroom. In fact, according to the National Women's History Museum, a teacher named Peggy Whitley was the first to be allowed to teach children while pregnant—in 1968.[6.6] There's no record of the first unmarried woman to teach while visibly pregnant, but not surprisingly, there are plenty of people who still don't think that's appropriate.

In the spring of 2012, for instance, 29-year-old Cathy Samford was fired by the Heritage Christian Academy in Rockwall, Texas, after becoming pregnant before marriage. Samford was engaged at the time, but that was not sufficient for the Academy's headmaster, Dr. Ron Taylor. "How's it going to look to a little fourth grade girl who sees that she's pregnant and not married?" Dr. Taylor asked one reporter. "We have a right to have standards of conduct[.]"[6.7]

Similarly, Jarretta Hamilton, a fourth-grade teacher at the Southland Christian School in St. Cloud, Florida, was fired when administrators figured out that she had conceived her child three months before getting married. Hamilton filed a federal lawsuit challenging the dismissal, and the 11th Circuit Court of Appeals ruled that Hamilton was entitled to a jury trial on the issue of whether Southland improperly discriminated against Hamilton on the basis of her pregnancy, as opposed to her violation of the school's religious principles.[6.8]

Hamilton no doubt is hoping for an outcome similar to that of Christa Dias, who was fired by her employer, the Roman Catholic Archdiocese in Cincinnati, after not only getting pregnant while unmarried, but doing so through artificial insemination. The Church argued that by using artificial insemination in violation of the Church's teachings, Dias had violated her contract. A jury disagreed, however, and awarded Dias $170,000 for pregnancy discrimination.[6.9]

For some religious schools (and politicians), merely shacking up is still sufficient to disqualify someone from teaching. In 2010, for instance, then-Senator Jim DeMint (R-S.C.) told pastors at the Greater Freedom Rally in Spartanburg, South Caroline that "if someone is openly homosexual, they shouldn't be teaching in the classroom and he holds the same position on an unmarried woman who's sleeping with her boyfriend—she shouldn't be in the classroom."[6.10]

In California, Sara Henry, a pre-school director for the Red Hill Evangelical Lutheran Church of Tustin was fired when it was discovered that she was living with her boyfriend,[6.11] as was Colorado's Ashlie Simpson. A student service adviser at Colorado Christian University, Simpson admitted to administrators that she was living with her boyfriend and was fired. Simpson has also filed a federal lawsuit, alleging that university officials inappropriately pressed her for information about her lifestyle and whether she was having sexual relations with her boyfriend.[6.12]

What should be evident from these examples is that there is still an enduring interest in the private lives of the nation's educators (and, it must be added, especially those of women). Clearly, much of society has moved well beyond the days when school boards felt like they had the right to mandate church attendance and limit a teacher's courtin' to just two nights a week. But the expectation that teachers will serve as positive role models for their students not only while in the classroom but also in their private lives has not faded significantly.

What HAS changed dramatically, however, is the ability of school boards, administrators, parents, and students to learn surprisingly detailed information about the private lives of teachers. A series of technological developments—the personal computer, the World Wide Web, mobile devices, and social media—has made it harder for educators to keep information private. As we'll see, some of that is beyond the control of individual educators; powerful search engines like Google and Bing can resurrect information about educators that they might have thought was long dead and buried, or publicize obscure opinions and writing that once would have remained hidden and largely unread.

At the same time, however, a significant portion of the loss of privacy experienced by educators is selfie-inflicted. The digital communication revolution of the past forty years has given educators (and of course, a host of other people) unprecedented opportunities to damage or even destroy their personal privacy. It is not unreasonable to think that the standards to which educators are held are unfair. But the reality is that those standards exist, and educators need to be particularly careful about how and when they use digital devices; the margin of error, never large, is growing steadily smaller.

~~~~~~~~~

Chapter Seven
The Risks of Posting Personal Opinions and Frustrations

Just about everyone has had at least one bad day at work, or a day when some combination of illness, depression, and interpersonal dyspepsia has left them out of sorts and just plain grumpy. For educators, that once might have led to a venting of snarky and even off-color student assessments in the privacy of the teacher's lounge, or in a long phone chat with a friend, or maybe over a consoling drink at a bar. But thanks to Mark Zuckerberg (and others, to be fair), teachers now have the option of grousing in very public ways. In fact, the very existence of Facebook and its widespread integration into our social lives arguably encourages us to share thoughts and impressions that we once would never have considered sharing, because they were impolitic, inane, mean-spirited, petty, or some combination of all of the above.

Not surprisingly, when educators publicly ridicule or grouse about their students, their parents typically take offense, and frequently demand that school officials fire the indiscreet educator. In some instances, they may go so far as to file a lawsuit against the offending teacher, administrators, the school district, and anyone else their lawyer can credibly put in the complaint.

"But I intended the comments to be private," an aggrieved educator will no doubt will protest. "I had my 'privacy' settings at the highest level!' That's terrific. But in the digital era, it's also basically meaningless. The basic message can't be reiterated too often: if something is posted online, the odds are very good that it WILL get out, one way or the other. Here's a trivial but telling example: The photo-sharing Web site Flickr allows its users to disable downloading for any or all photos stored on the site. That feature prevents Web surfers from simply right-clicking and saving a restricted photo to their computer. But it's a relatively simple matter to perform a screen capture of any photo on the Web, regardless of the download setting. The same is true for virtually every other type of information online.

Most educators who get into trouble over indiscreet posts are not the victim of even low-level data scraping like screen captures. It's much more common for the data leakage to occur because the comments were intentionally or accidentally made available to the entire Web. For example, Dr. June Talvitie-Siple, the program supervisor for math and science at Cohasset High School in Plymouth County, Massachusetts, posted a series of public messages on her Facebook page. She had pithy things to say about Cohasset parents ("so arrogant and snobby"), the 2010-2011 school year ("so not looking forward to another year at Cohasset Schools"), and her disease-inducing students ("Now I remember why I stopped teaching! Kids … they are all germ bags!"). The day after the comments were posted, Dr. Talvitie-Siple was asked to resign from her $92,636-a-year job.[71]

In a subsequent interview, Dr. Talvitie-Siple said that she had simply made a mistake: "There [*sic*] weren't meant for the rest of the world. Most of it was a joke and my friends would have understood that. I didn't think it was a public Facebook page."[7.2]

Most educators are aware (or at least should be) that if they post something publicly, even by accident, then they need to deal with the consequences of doing so. But what if he or she HAS double-checked the privacy settings and triple-checked to make sure that only "friends" can see the latest dyspeptic summary of life? An old German proverb sums it up best: *Behüte mich Gott vor meinen Freunden, mit den Feinden will ich schon fertig werden* ("God preserve me from my friends, I can deal with my enemies").[7.3] And all too often overlooked is the fact that Facebook has badly diluted the meaning of the word "friend." Is the 200th person on a person's Facebook friend list really a "friend," or just someone to impress with jealousy-inducing vacation photos?

This dilution of the concept of "friend" can have real-life consequences. If an educator makes an uncharitable or unkind comment to an actual friend over a cup of coffee, he or she can have some degree of confidence that it will be kept private. But if that same educator broadcasts the same comment to 300 Facebook friends, the odds are very good that one or more of them will feel no obligation to keep it confidential. That is essentially what happened to Jennifer O'Brien, a first-grade teacher at School 21 in Paterson, New Jersey. After a particularly bad day at work, which she later said involved persistent student disruption, an assault, and theft, she told her 333 Facebook friends that "I'm not a teacher—I'm a warden for future criminals!"[7.4]

O'Brien's comment was forwarded by some Facebook friends to others, and the following day, a "significant" number of parents came to her school, demanding that she be fired. The administration agreed, and the decision was upheld by an administrative law judge, who described O'Brien's conduct as "inexcusable." In a statement, Paterson School Board President Theodore Best summarized the reasons for the district's actions: "The reason why she was suspended was because the incident created serious problems at the school that impeded the functioning of the building. You can't simply fire someone for what they have on a Facebook page; but if that spills over and affects the classroom then you can take action."[7.5]

Another example of this social media cybertrap is the case of Dana Fitzpatrick, a computer teacher at the Anthony Overton Elementary School in Chicago. In 2011, 7-year-old Ukailya Lofton's unusual hair-do so amazed Fitzpatrick that she asked the young girl if she could take some photos. Lofton's mother, Lucinda Williams, had seen photos of a celebrity with Jolly Rancher candies dangling from the end of her braids, and she recreated the hairstyle for Lofton's school photo day. But when Lofton told her mother that Fitzpatrick had taken her photo, Williams decided to check the teacher's Facebook page.[7.6]

Williams discovered that Fitzpatrick had posted the photos with the caption "right, this is for picture day." Various Facebook friends added their own critical opinions, ranging from "if you are going to make your child look ridiculous, the least you can do is have them matching," to "yeah, this is foolishness," to "I laughed so hard that my contact popped out." Williams told a local television station that the teacher had deleted the photos and comments from Facebook and apologized to her, but not to her daughter.[77] On April 6, 2011, Williams filed a lawsuit against the Chicago Board of Education and Dana Fitzpatrick, seeking $29,000 in damages for intentional infliction of emotional distress to her daughter. The lawsuit was eventually dismissed in 2012, but Fitzpatrick did receive a Warning Resolution from the Chicago Board of Education for "unsatisfactory conduct."[78]

Probably the most highly-publicized example of educator oversharing on Facebook involves Christina Rubino, a New York City 5th grade teacher. For three years, Rubino was embroiled in a long-running dispute with the state Department of Education over ill-advised comments that she made on Facebook in the summer of 2010. After a particularly tumultuous day in the classroom, Rubino used her Blackberry to post a very critical comment about her class: "After today, I'm thinking the beach sounds like a wonderful idea for my 5th graders. I HATE THEIR GUTS! They are all the devils spawn!" When one of her friends jokingly commented, "oh you would let little Kwame float away!" Rubino replied "Yes, I wld not throw a life jacket in for a million!!"[7.9]

Rubino's comments were incendiary by themselves, but what made her Facebook post particularly upsetting to some was that a 12-year-old girl from Harlem, Nicole Suriel, had drowned the day before while on a field trip to a Long Island beach. Upset by what he read, Rubino's colleague and Facebook friend David Senatore printed out the exchange and took it to school administrators. Rubino was summarily fired, a move that was upheld by arbitrator Randi Lowitt on the grounds that Rubino had exhibited conduct unbecoming a teacher. "Social media, Facebook, LinkedIn, Twitter, all these and more are becoming embedded in society," Lowitt said in his opinion. "People post without regard to the fact that what they post has a shelf life of forever."[7.10]

Rubino filed a lawsuit challenging her dismissal, and a state court judge overruled the arbitrator, find that while Rubino's remarks were "offensive" and "repulsive," termination was too severe a penalty. The arbitrator was ordered to reconsider the case, and he gave Rubino a two-year suspension, a ruling that ultimately cost her approximately $150,000 in lost salary and benefits. Rubino appealed that decision as well, but the suspension was upheld.

In the meantime, the Department of Education appealed the state court ruling, but lost on appeal. A four-judge panel of the NY State Appellate Decision affirmed the lower court ruling and seemed to suggest that educators might be entitled to a "zone of privacy" even online. "Although the comments were clearly inappropriate," the appellate court said, "it is apparent that petitioner's purpose was to vent her frustration only to her online friends after a difficult day with her own students."[7.11]

It is entirely possible that over the next few years, societal attitudes towards online temper tantrums may ease, or that privacy controls will grow sufficiently sophisticated to allow educators to carefully limit what they post to a small, trusted group of real "friends." But in the interim, every educator should think long and hard about what they post online, and never forget that what is digital is easily copied. If it's not something that can be said or shown at a PTA meeting, then maybe it's not fit for social media.

~~~~~~~~~

Frederick S. Lane

Chapter Eight
The Rickety Soap Box: Political Opinions and Social Commentary

As the results rolled in on Election Night 2012, a disappointed teacher at Linden McKinley High School in Columbus, Ohio logged onto Facebook to sarcastically applaud the outcome:

> Congrats to those dependent on government, homosexuals, potheads, JAY-Z fans, non Christians, non taxpayers, illegals, communists, Muslims, planned murder clinics, enemies of America, Satan You WON!

Although the comment was posted to the teacher's personal Facebook page, news of the incendiary post quickly spread, and at least one parent printed out a copy to share with the school's principal. The district launched an investigation, but since no formal action was taken, the name of the teacher was not publicized. As one parent pointed out, however, it was a particularly insensitive comment for a teacher working in a school where 95 percent of the students are on free and reduced lunch.[8.1]

A few hundred miles away in Oklahoma City, a high school science teacher named Lamont Lowe was equally upset by the news that residents of the state of Oklahoma had approved a referendum banning affirmative action programs in the state. His Facebook post was equally scathing:

> I live in a state that hates me, hates women…revoking affirmative action is spitting in my face. This is the reason I hate OU Sooners and the OKC Thunder, and everything that represents this racist state! Die Oklahoma! Hope a tornado blows away the Capital and all the rednecks in it.

Not surprisingly, the post attracted a lot of negative attention, and some parents argued that he should be terminated. The Oklahoma City school district, however, declined to take any action and issued a statement that read: "OKCPS is very disappointed and saddened by the teacher's post. We do not agree with or support his comments. But we do recognize his first amendment right to freedom of speech." Lowe subsequently apologized for his choice of words and said that in fact, he did not hate Oklahomans.[8.2]

Not every teacher who makes controversial statements gets to keep his or her job, of course. Most recently, Angela Box, a third-grade teacher in the Houston Independent School District ("HISD"), handed in her resignation following controversy over comments she made while appearing on "Tommy's Garage," a conservative cable access television show in Houston. Among other things, Box denigrated Muslims ("Every normal human being in the world knows that goat-fucking Muslims and, oh, boy fucking Muslims, are the evil of the world.") and joked about Ebola killing President Obama ("Can't Ebola just take one for the team and take out Obama?").[8.3]

The HISD took no action against Box for her comments, saying that it respected her First Amendment rights. However, when Box submitted her resignation, the HISD Board of Trustees accepted it unanimously and gave Box three month's severance pay.[8.4]

It is important for teachers to keep in mind that in cases like these, a school district does not have to accept a resignation and allow a teacher to quietly fade into the night. On Friday, November 7, 2014, at the height of the anticipation over the grand jury decision regarding the slaying of Michael Brown, Texas teacher Vinita Hegwood used her personal Twitter account to make a particularly emphatic statement:

Who the fuck made you dumb duck ass crackers think I give a squat fuck about your opinions about my opinions RE: #Ferguson? Kill yourselves.

Not surprisingly, the tweet attracted a lot of attention from students, parents, and administrators in the Duncanville Independent School District ("DISD"), and Sunday evening, the District was promising swift action:

As an individual, Ms. Vinita Hegwood expressed an opinion on social media that is solely her own. She used her personal social media account to make remarks that are offensive. While everyone has the right to free speech, as a teacher in the district, we believe the comments that are alleged to be made by Ms. Hegwood are absolutely reprehensible and we do not condone it.

The district is taking swift action in this matter within the authority set forth by district policy. Duncanville ISD embraces diversity and is not defined by the personal opinion of one.[8.5]

The District kept its word, placing Hegwood on administrative leave without pay on Monday morning pending further investigation. Three days later, Hegwood handed in her resignation and issued a public apology:

I wish to express my regret regarding the controversy over comments that I made on social media on Friday, November 7. I am deeply sorry for the offensive and unprofessional comments that I made on my personal Twitter account. In making those remarks, I was reacting to a series of threatening and racist attacks against me by strangers who disagreed with my expressed opinions on Ferguson, Missouri. I allowed myself to respond emotionally and impulsively. My reaction in no way reflects the standards to which I have held myself and my students for the last twenty years of teaching. I accept full responsibility for my actions, and I regret the embarrassment that it has caused the school district. I believe that it is in the best interests of the district that I resign my position at Duncanville ISD effective immediately.[8.6]

At a special meeting held on the morning of November 14, however, the DISD voted to reject Hegwood's resignation and terminate her contract instead.[8.7]

Taken together, these cases (and dozens like them) raise the legitimate question of whether teachers are entitled to First Amendment protection for the things they say. Theoretically, the answer to that question is still "yes," particularly if the teacher in question works in a public school (teachers who work in private schools have less protection because the Constitution and Bill of Rights do not apply to businesses and corporations). However, in 2006, the United States Supreme Court established a two-part test for determining whether statements by a public employee are entitled to First Amendment protection: 1) was the statement made as a private citizen about a matter of public concern, or as an employee about matters within the scope of his or her employment; and 2) did the state employer have an "adequate" reason for treating the employee differently than a member of the general public? Put another way, did the speech unduly interfere with the ability of the state employer to operate effectively?[8.8]

One of the consequences of the Court's decision has been a steady weakening of educator First Amendment protection. It is a classic Catch-22: if a teacher is speaking about something determined to be within the scope of his or her employment, or is commenting on something that is not considered to be of public concern, then there is no First Amendment protection. On the other hand, even if a teacher is speaking as a private citizen about an significant public issue (such as the death of Michael Brown), he or she can still be denied First Amendment protection if the school district concludes that the speech is too disruptive to the operation of the district or to the school environment. The net effect, then, is that First Amendment protection can only reliably be enjoyed by public school teachers who make non-controversial statements about subjects that have nothing to do with their professional responsibilities.

Ideally, the Court will reconsider its decision at some point in the future. But in the meantime, educators should be cognizant of the fact that media (particularly social media) has an amplifying effect that makes it far too easy for school boards and school districts to claim that a teacher's speech is disruptive. There is no question, for instance, that when Hegwood decided to post her angry message to Twitter, it became a much bigger deal than it would have been had she merely shouted it at a group of people walking past her house. The sad fact is that in the current legal climate, educators should think carefully about the instantaneous, global nature of social media and the durability of digital information. Keep in mind that even though Hegwood deleted her Twitter account before attempting to resign, there are an endless number of screen shots of her tweet online.

~~~~~~~~

Chapter Nine
Posting Inappropriate Photos and Videos

As American writer Stewart Brand said at a Hacker's Conference in 1984, "Information wants to be free." Brand was referring at the time to the ever-dropping cost of distributing information (thus implicitly foreseeing the shake-up of content industries like movies, music, and books), but the alternative meaning is also true: Information wants to be "free" as in "unfettered" and "unconfined." Anyone who's ever told a secret knows this. When you post a digital photo, even with so-called privacy protections in place, it's a closely-held secret that you're sharing with your 200, 400, or 800 closest friends—and each of *their* numerous friends. You can do the math: only one of those thousands of extended "friends" needs to take offense at your photo, and a potential nightmare will begin.

For example: In the summer of 2009, Ashley Payne, a teacher at Appalachee High School in Barrow County, Georgia went on an enjoyable trip to various places in Europe. When she returned home, she created an album on Facebook of about 700 photos, precisely ten of which showed Payne drinking alcohol. One showed her sipping from a foaming glass of Guinness, and another showed her holding half-empty glasses of wine and beer in her hands. Sometime after returning home, she also posted that she was heading out to play "Crazy Bitch Bingo," a game popular with a number of establishments in the area in which she lived. Payne's Facebook privacy settings were set to a very high level, and the album was only available to a small group of Payne's acquaintances.

On the morning of August 27, Payne's superintendent, Dr. Ron Saunders, received an anonymous email informing him of the contents of Payne's Facebook page, and asserting that the writer's daughter had started using the slang term "bitches" (as in "female friends") because of Payne's Facebook posts. Attached to the email was a copy of the photo showing D'Amico holding up two glasses of alcohol. The email concluded: "I am repulsed by Ms. Payne's profane use of language and how she conducts herself as an example to my teenage daughter. Her behavior is intolerable. I have a question to the Barrow County School System. Is it too hard for our educators to lack [*sic*] discipline online and offline? I have chosen to remain anonymous regarding this matter for the sake of my daughter."[9.1]

As Atlanta Journal-Constitution reporter Maureen Downey noted, the grammatically-perfect email (with proper business memo formatting to boot) contained one significant factual error: none of Payne's students were Friends with her on Facebook, and Payne insisted there were no errors in her privacy settings. Downey tried to contact the writer but the email had been sent from a temporary anonymous email account that was no longer active.[9.2]

Regardless of the source of email (Downey speculated that it was a hostile co-worker), the outcome for Payne was draconian. Just two hours after the email was received, Superintendent Saunders confronted Payne and told her that the combination of photos showing alcohol use and foul language on her Facebook page made it impossible for her to keep her job. She was given the option of resigning on the spot or receiving a suspension that would be on her permanent teaching record.[9.3] Payne resigned, but then later filed a lawsuit in Georgia state court, alleging that she had been unlawfully terminated. However, the Piedmont Circuit Court issued summary judgment in favor of the school district in April 2013. Multiple news sources reported that Payne, by then a graduate student at the University of Georgia, was planning to appeal the lower court's decision.[9.4]

Payne's case is a classic example of how even relatively innocuous content can get an educator in trouble, depending on the sensitivity of the district in question. It also illustrates how difficult it can be, even with international media support, to overturn a disciplinary action or termination.

If Payne is a leading contender for most sympathetic victim of social media oversharing, then Colorado's Carly McKinney has a solid headlock on least. The 23-year-old was a math teacher at Overland High School in Aurora, Colorado, when a local television station received a tip that McKinney was posting inappropriate material on Twitter under the handle "@CrunkBear."[9.5] The Twitter ID itself was arguably inappropriate for a high school teacher; the Urban Dictionary defines the word "crunk" variously as "crazy drunk" or "high AND drunk."[9.6]

Regardless, it was the content of McKinney's posts and the attached photos that started tongues wagging and administrators frowning. Here are a few samples, which were captured by Denver's 9News before the Twitter account was made private and then shut down altogether:

- "@SpliffMeister All day every day... unless you're a teacher like me. Then you just wait for after school."
- "#SpliffManiac Nothing better than medical marijuana."
- "My favorite □ http://t.co/C3Dd7dQ5 " (the attached photo showed McKinney smoking some substance in her car)
- "Sleep naked. Good night twitter. Sweet muthafuckin dreamzzzzz http://t.co/0RjAoCQi " (the attached photo showed McKinney lying face down on her bed, apparently naked, with a blanket just barely covering her rear end)
- "Just got called Ms. McCutie. Points for being clever, however you are still jailbait."
- "Naked. Wet. Stoned"
- "Watching a drug bust go down in the parking lot. It's funny cuz I have weed in my car in the staff parking lot."

Other provocative photos on McKinney's Twitter feed included: a selfie of her torso in just a thin t-shirt and underwear, showing her "framp stamp," a tattoo on or just above the vaginal area;[9.7] a topless mirror selfie with McKinney holding her hands across her breasts; and a shot of McKinney doing a topless handstand on her bed in a black thong, with her back to the camera.

In response to the reports about McKinney's Twitter feed, Overland High School administrators put her on paid leave while they conducted an investigation. McKinney told school officials that the Twitter account was intended as a parody, and that she shared the administration of the account with a "friend," who was the one responsible for the more provocative posts. (Left unexplained was how the "friend" obtained the selfies showing McKinney in various stages of undress). To be fair, none of McKinney's tweets were actually illegal (even the pictures are at most PG-13), and recreational marijuana use is legal in Colorado. Nonetheless, Overland administrators called in the Aurora police to determine whether McKinney had brought pot onto the school campus, which is still prohibited. The results of the investigation were inconclusive, and McKinney was not charged.[9.8] As of March 2013, McKinney was no longer an employee of the Cherry Creek School District, either through resignation or termination (the exact terms of her departure is unclear).[9.9]

As an expression of solidarity with McKinney, many students at Overland (as well as supportive individuals around the world) began tweeting the hash tag "#FreeCrunkBear" and wearing t-shirts protesting her firing.[9.10] The campaign enjoyed a brief flurry of media attention in early 2013, but has since largely disappeared. Certainly, it had no discernible impact on the school district's position regarding McKinney's fitness to teach.

Not every case involving indiscreet online photos has ended badly for the educator involved. A few years ago, Ginger D'Amico, a Spanish teacher in the Brownsville (PA) Area School District, was at a bachelorette party, and someone took a photo that showed D'Amico laughing and pushing away a male stripper. The photo was posted to a friend's Facebook page, and was reported to school administrators by someone in the community. All of the teachers who attended the party were given letters of reprimand, except for D'Amico. Because hers was the only face that could be identified in the photo, she was given a 30-day suspension. Backed by the local branch of the ACLU, D'Amico threatened to file suit. The school district agreed to settle the matter by paying D'Amico $10,000, a $4,400 reimbursement for back pay, and expungement of the disciplinary action from her record.[9,11]

Teachers who use social media regularly, however, should not rely on one favorable outcome among a sea of negative responses. Over time, cultural and social mores will change, and school districts may grow more comfortable with teachers sharing aspects of their personal social lives online. But in the interim, educators should think carefully before clicking "send."

~~~~~~~~~

Chapter Ten
Risqué Second Jobs

One of the painful realities of teaching is that it frequently doesn't pay very well, particularly when you are first starting out, and the Great Recession made things significantly more difficult. It's not uncommon, then, for teachers and administrators to pick up a second job over the summer (or even at night during the school year) to help make ends meet: My family and I, for instance, would occasionally see my son's fifth grade teacher at the Italian restaurant where she worked two or three nights a week (which, much to my son's dismay, gave us a chance to have bonus parent-teacher conferences). She was not alone. According to the *Huffington Post*, over twenty percent of the nation's teachers were working two or more jobs in 2011.

While the percentage ebbs and flows from year to year, there's nothing new about educators working extra jobs, nor is there anything particularly new about the fact that it really does matter what type of additional work you choose to do. For educators, picking up some extra money as a stripper or adult film star today is just as frowned upon today as it would have been to work evenings as a Playboy Bunny 50 years ago or dance weekends as a flapper in a 1920s nightclub. The problem for educators today, however, is that the odds of being discovered are so much higher: first, the Internet has made it far easier (and tempting) for educators to test the old maxim that "sex sells," in all its myriad forms (or at least pays well); and second, the Internet has made it much harder to do so surreptitiously or anonymously. What the Web giveth, the Web taketh away.

My research for this book over the last couple of years suggests that if anything, school districts and school boards are much quicker these days to take disciplinary action against a teacher who is "outed" online for risqué or explicit activity for one simple reason: kids now have easy access to all of the same information, Web sites, Twitter feeds, and other electronic resources that adults do. In fact, most kids are far more attuned to the buzz of the Internet than adults, and generally much more adept at locating information. The practical outcome is that this type of news is now much more likely to erode a teacher's moral authority with students and cause disruption in the classroom. Once the Internet echo chamber has been fired up, it's very difficult for district administrators or school board members to ignore the noise and defend a wayward educator who's walking (let alone streetwalking) on the wild side.

In the digital world in which we live, an educator's zone of privacy is microscopically small and steadily shrinking. It raises the question, not easily answered, of just how risqué can a second job be before it's a problem in the classroom.

For instance, should a teacher be fired for picking up a little extra cash as a waitress at Hooter's? 24-year-old Nicole Zivitch, the cheerleading coach for Estero High School in Florida's Lee County School District, was fired on November

21, 2011 after the parent of one of her cheerleaders wrote over 200 emails to the school board and superintendent, complaining about her after-hours work.[10.1] Among other things, the parent described Zivich as "[an] inexperienced 24 year old Hooters waitress" who lacked "maturity and judgment."[10.2]

The district denied that Zivich was terminated for working at Hooter's, but declined to give a reason for the coach's termination, saying that a supplemental contract (as is typically given to activity coordinators who are not also teachers) can be revoked at any time without cause.[10.3] However, Zivich may have had the last laugh. Following the reports of her termination, Zivich appeared on "Anderson Cooper 360" and "Inside Edition," and was hired to run an all-star high school cheerleading squad by a local fitness club, Xtreme Air Sports. Eleven underclassmen tried out for her squad and eight seniors quit the Estero High squad, leaving just four remaining cheerleaders.[10.4]

How about posing for photographs in a bikini (or a little less)? On April 29, 2013, the principal of the Martin County High School in Boca Raton, Florida summoned English teacher Olivia Sprauer to his office and handed her a printout out of a Web page showing a skimpily-dressed model posing for a business called <u>XXXTremeMusicTelevision</u>. When Sprauer conceded that she had been working part-time as a so-called "eye-candy model" (posing in bikinis and lingerie) for the site, she was asked to resign and leave the school immediately.[10.5]

Based on an interview she gave at the time, it was pretty clear that Sprauer knew there was a risk her part-time job might cause problems with the school district. "I knew it was either [*sic*] a matter of time," she told veteran Florida reporter Al Pefley. "I'm surprised it didn't happen earlier actually. I started modeling mid-February [2013]." A divorced mother of two small children, Sprauer said that she planned to continue modeling under her stage name, <u>Victoria James</u>. She pointed out that she could make as much money in a single weekend of modeling as she could in two weeks in the classroom.[10.6]

One particularly notorious case of a risqué second job involved Tiffany Shepherd, a single mother of three boys and a well-liked biology teacher at Port St. Lucie High School in the St. Lucie County School District in Florida. In 2008, needing some extra income after a difficult divorce, Shepherd took a part-time job as a "bikini hostess" for the now-defunct Smokin' Em Charters. The company advertised full and half-day fishing trips accompanied by bikini-clad and occasionally topless waitresses. Like the other hostesses, Shepherd was featured on the company's Web site wearing various bikinis; one photo showed her lying face down and topless on the deck of a boat. In an interview with ABC News, Shepherd (a life-long angler) described it as a perfect job: "I wasn't making enough money," she said. "This was perfect because I could get paid to fish. It was easy money. In two days fishing, I make more than I do in a week teaching." She strenuously denied ever working topless, although she admitted that she would occasionally go topless on private trips.[10.7]

Shepherd worked her first trip for Smokin' Em Charters on April 19, 2008, and four days later, was fired from her teaching job. The district alleged that Shepherd had excessive absences, and that it was unaware of her working as a bikini hostess when it let her go. Shepherd told ABC News that rumors about her new gig had begun to circulate among school board members and even students before she was fired, and blamed the notoriety accompanying her online photos for her firing.[10.8]

You might be thinking that none of these teachers should have been terribly surprised that their risqué second jobs were discovered, and that they led to disciplinary action. In our increasingly interconnected world, the chances of keeping that type of information a secret, particularly from the tech-savvy, hormone-suffused, Internet gurus that inhabit every high school, are incredibly low. When salacious information emerges, it now spreads at the speed of light. But what is coming as a shock to more than a few teachers is the fact that thanks to the voracious appetite of the Internet and search engines for information, even long-forgotten risqué jobs can suddenly re-emerge from the depths of the past.

Consider, for instance, the case of Tiffani Webb, a guidance counselor at the Murry Bergtraum HS for Business Careers in Manhattan. In December 2011, a student allegedly gave Webb's principal, Andrea Lewis, a printout of a Web page showing Webb in revealing lingerie. Despite the fact that Webb was a well-liked and accomplished counselor, and notwithstanding the fact that she was just days away from receiving tenure after twelve years of successful employment, she was fired for "conduct unbecoming" an employee of the Department of Education.[10.9]

What made Webb's termination even more questionable was the fact that the photos had been taken in the early to mid-1990s, but were still floating around the Internet nearly 20 years later. In some instances, she said, the photos had been Photoshopped or otherwise altered, and were used without permission as advertising on a variety of Web sites. Moreover, Webb had told the Department of Education about her past modeling career, and despite three internal investigations, had not been disciplined in any way. In fact, she received nothing but satisfactory ratings for her work over the course of her career.[10.10]

Webb appealed her dismissal but lost by a 2-1 vote. The key language of the ruling underscores just how little margin for error there is for educators today: "The inappropriate photos were accessible to impressionable adolescents," the decision said. "That behavior has a potentially adverse influence on her ability to counsel students and be regarded as a role model."[10.11]

Two months after her dismissal, Webb—now known as Tiffani Notre Ellis—filed suit against the New York City Department of Education, alleging that her firing was a violation of her First Amendment rights. Her complaint asked for an award of "lost wages, costs, and damages for pain and suffering, loss of reputation and constitutional violations."[10.12] A motion by the Department of Education to dismiss Ellis's claim for failure to state a cause of action was rejected by the Kings County Supreme Court on July 3, 2012, and the case is still pending.[10.13]

The need to work a second job is a painful reality for many educators, and there is little question that risqué jobs often pay better than more buttoned-up alternatives. However, even though all of the jobs discussed in this chapter are legal, most school districts and many parents are still concerned about the example teachers set for their students. Whether an educator should take the risk of choosing a risqué second job is ultimately up to them, but for the time being, no one should be surprised if it quickly leads to an uncomfortable conversation with the school principal or district administrators.

~~~~~~~~~

Chapter Eleven
Posting Sexually Explicit Photos and Videos

It may come as a shock to some school boards, but the educators that they hire do have sex. Not only that, but those same educators have a range of sexual proclivities and interests that mirrors the rest of society, running the gamut from the blandest vanilla to the most profoundly kinky. It is a dead certainty that over the course of the past century, teachers have written dirty notes to spouses, taken or posed for nude photographs, and even made the occasional home sex film or tape. In the pre-Internet era, those peccadilloes were much less likely to come to light and cause problems for the educator or the school district. Notwithstanding the prurient interest shown by some politicians and school administrations, most school boards generally adhere to the philosophy of British actress Beatrice Campbell (1865-1940), who upon hearing a whispered bit of gossip that a fellow actor might be gay, famously replied "My dear, I don't care what they do, so long as they don't do it in the street and frighten the horses."

The Internet has changed social mores in myriad ways, but perhaps nothing has been quite so startling as the willingness, if not the downright enthusiasm of average folks to risk scaring the horses by publishing nude and sexually explicit images of themselves online. It's no great surprise that digital camera technology increased the number of people who took sexy photos or recorded themselves having sex for their own pleasure—digital cameras make it fast, discreet, and basically free, so why not? But without a doubt, the real eye-opener has been the increase in the number of people willing to SHARE such photos online. It's hard to imagine the average educator thirty or forty years ago taking his or her collection of nude Polaroids or snapshots and posting them on bulletin boards around the community. But for all intents and purposes, that's what some educators are doing when they share nude photos of themselves on the Internet.

The modern corollary of Campbell's statement for educators is that most school boards won't care what you do so long as it doesn't disrupt the school environment (although there are definitely exceptions in some of the more conservative parts of the country). As we'll see, however, the Internet has made that a MUCH lower threshold than it used to be, particularly given the fact that the population most likely to be disrupted by a teacher's risqué or outré Facebook posts—his or her students—are also probably the most likely to find them.

There is a dizzying array of ways in which these supposedly private images can become public. In some instances, it's a combination of sheer bad luck and what Sacramento defense attorney Ken Rosenfeld wittily described as "felony stupidity."[11.1] One all-too-common example in this category is the case of Paul Withee, a math and science teacher and highly-regarded football coach at the Oxford

Middle School in Oxford, ME. In February 2012, Withee posted a nude photo of himself to Facebook; he intended the photo to be privately viewed by a friend, but instead mistakenly made the photo public. Despite the fact that the image was only public for ten minutes before Withee realized his mistake, a parent saw the photo and reported it to district officials. Withee resigned his position after meeting with District Superintendent Rick Colpitts.[11.2]

In an interview with *Bangor Daily News* reporter Leslie H. Dixon, Withee gave a poignant summation of the consequences of his mistake. "I'm embarrassed, I'm ashamed, I'm humiliated," he said. "I've never done anything like this before and I never will again. You have to be careful with what you do with social media. You can get yourself into a lot of trouble and something you love can be taken away from you just like this."[11.3]

Withee has lots of company. Just ask Crystal Defanti, a fifth grade teacher at the Isabelle Jackson Elementary School in Sacramento, California. In the spring of 2009, she prepared a year-end DVD with video clips of class projects, field trips, *etc.*, and sent a copy home with each student. Later that evening, Defanti learned that when she copied videos from her computer onto the DVDs, she accidentally included a six-second clip of a home sex tape that she had made of herself on the living room couch.[11.4] According to one parent, Defanti "called his home the day after his child got the DVD, crying hysterically, profusely apologizing and asking the man and his wife to call every parent they knew to stop their kids from seeing the DVD too."[11.5]

The school's reaction was surprisingly understanding. An investigation was launched to determine how the explicit material was included in the DVD, but there was no outcry among parents for Defanti's dismissal. A spokeswoman for the school advised parents to destroy the DVD distributed by Defanti and said that a new version would be sent out "once it had been reviewed."[11.6] It's not clear whether the school district took any disciplinary action; the only thing that is certain is that Defanti is not currently listed as a member of the staff at the Isabelle Jackson Elementary School.

Far less understanding were the administrators at the Cincinnati Hills Christian Academy, who discovered in late November 2013 that various private photos (including two nude selfies) of a fifth-grade teacher at the school had been published on at least three adult Web sites. The school declined to name the teacher, but various media outlets subsequently identified her as Jaime Climie, a wife and mother of 2 living in the Cincinnati area. Climie told school officials that she had no idea how the photos had made it to the Web; the day after the photos were discovered, she reported to police that her iPhone had been stolen.[11.7]

The school placed Climie on paid leave on December 2, and she resigned from the school the following weekend as news of the photos began to spread. Although it was undoubtedly small comfort, the owner of one of the Web sites that published her photos was arrested a couple of days later.

Kevin Christopher Bollaert, 27, was the creator of a "revenge porn" site called "ugotposted.com," which featured more than 10,000 sexually explicit photos. He was charged by California Attorney General Kamala D. Harris with 31 counts of conspiracy, identity theft, and extortion (Bollaert ran a second site on which he offered to remove photos from ugotposted.com if victims agreed to pay up to $350).[11.8]

In 2011, administrators and parents at Kingsway Elementary School in Charlotte County, Florida, received copies of an explicit video showing teacher Natalie Santagata in "various compromising acts." The video also depicted Santagata smoking marijuana. District Superintendent Douglas Whittaker told the school board that Santagata should be fired for "'personal conduct (or misconduct)' that 'clearly rises to the statutory standard of moral turpitude.'"[11.9]

What makes the Santagata case interesting is that she was summarily fired despite playing no role at all in the distribution of the video. USB thumb drives containing a copy of the video were delivered anonymously to school district officials and several parents received links to the video in their Facebook accounts. Superintendent Whittaker told a local television station: "It's a judgment call as to what goes on in a person's private life, as to have impact on their credibility and effectiveness in the classroom. When anonymous information comes in with photos and video that gives proof to what is claimed, we have to pay attention to that." In the end, Whittaker concluded, "[The video] directly impacted her ability to be an effective teacher in the classroom."[11,10]

The malicious release of Santagata's home sex video is an example of the growing phenomenon of "revenge porn," in which estranged spouses or disgruntled ex-lovers post explicit photos and videos on one or more of the myriad online Web sites that traffic in such content. It's no longer sufficient for educators to think twice about the images and videos that they themselves post online; you also need to be very confident that the person with whom you are lustily videotaping will not someday decide to post your naughty bits for the whole World Wide Web to see, or simply drop them off at your principal or superintendent's office.

~~~~~~~~~~

Chapter Twelve
Work in the Adult Entertainment Industry

In the broader swath of American society, the adult industry has lost a significant chunk of the social stigma that it once had. What was once a collection of underground enterprises rarely discussed in polite society is now a source of sitcom plots, fashion ideas (so-called "porn chic"), and technological innovation (streaming video and online credit card processing, among others). We've even had a United States Senator who posed nude, albeit with a strategically-placed hand, in a national magazine: Republican and Tea Party-darling Scott Brown, who recreated Burt Reynolds's famous *Playgirl* pose after being named "America's Sexiest Man" by *Cosmopolitan* in June 1982.[12.1] Adult film stars are finding it increasingly easy to cross over to the mainstream: Sibel Kikelli in the smash hit "Game of Thrones," James Deen in a highly-touted appearance in "The Canyons," and Sasha Gray in "The Girlfriend Experience" are just a few examples. And not surprisingly, tech companies have no problem hiring engineers and programmers with experience working on large, high-traffic porn Web sites.

Given all that, should someone with past experience in the adult industry be permanently barred from working as a teacher? After all, not only is it a legal activity, but it's constitutionally protected as well; thanks to a 1988 decision by the California Supreme Court, porn stars have a clear First

Amendment right to engage in on-screen sexual activity.[12.2] But once again, the Internet is making things much harder for educators and future educators than it used to be. Until the mid-1990s, what happened in the adult industry tended to stay in the adult industry; if a young person posed nude or even made one or two adult films and then sometime later decided to become a teacher, particularly in a different part of the country, the chances were fairly low that anyone would uncover the X-rated materials.

Increasingly, however, all of the flotsam and jetsam of our lives trails behind us online, like our own personal Great Pacific Garbage Patch. We have search engines, and especially Google, to thank for that: The headline on Google's company overview page states that the company's express "mission is to organize the world's information and make it universally accessible and useful."[12.3] The information that Google is trying to make "universally accessible and useful" comes from an almost infinite variety of sources: media outlets, professional Web sites, historical archives of one kind or another, databases, social media sites, and of course, whatever individuals and organizations decide to put on the Web.

That's terrific when someone like my art historian wife Amy is researching 19th century newspapers that have been scanned and digitized, but it's less terrific when the "information" in question are nude photos from a modeling session someone did to earn some extra cash while putting himself or herself through school, or a long-forgotten but brief foray into adult films. We're entering the third decade of the widely-adopted Web, so all of us need to think back to all the people, organizations, groups, and businesses with whom we've interacted or had dealings with over the last twenty-plus years. Any or all of them might have information—text, photos, videos—that they conceivably could post somewhere on the Internet for search engines to index and make accessible. And if any of the information that someone has about you involves sex, the odds of that information finding its way online increase significantly. This is one of the reasons I recommend that people routine Google themselves; it's not narcissism, it's just good sense.

The stark reality is that regardless of the growing tolerance for porn work in tech, film, and Congress, there is no statute of limitations when it comes to educators. I doubt that there is a single school board or school administrator in the country that would hire a known former porn star as a teacher or would continue to employ that person once his or her past employment was discovered. And as is the case with bikini or lingerie photos, it doesn't make much difference how long ago the adult industry work occurred; from a school district's perspective, old nude photos or porn film clips are just as disruptive today as they would have been when they were first made.

The experience of Texan Cristy Nicole Deweese is fairly typical. Shortly after the 21-year-old Deweese began teaching Spanish at the Rosie M. Collins Sorrells School of Education and Social Services in the Dallas Independent School District in the fall of 2013, some of her students did what students everywhere now do: they Googled their new teacher to learn more about her. One of the things that the students learned was that three years earlier, Deweese had posed as a model for Playboy.com under the name "Cristy Nicole" in part to earn some money to pay for her teaching certificate in Spanish language education.[12.4] Unfortunately, her teacher training program apparently did not alert her to the fact that her appearance on the Playboy.com Web site might prove problematic when she finished her training.

It's unclear who first discovered Deweese's *Playboy* gig, but based on the comments for the trailer for Deweese's video shoot, two or three students stumbled across the video in the fall of 2013 (each writing some variant of "That's my Spanish teacher!!"). Not surprisingly, the link to her*Playboy.com* video on YouTube and copies of photos from her February 2011 "Coed of the Month" photo spread began flying around the school.[12.5]

One parent, speaking anonymously, said that she was upset that Deweese had not been immediately removed from the classroom when DISD officials learned about her nude modeling past. "Are her male 16- and 17-year-old students looking at her without picturing her nude?" she asked. "And for the female students, is this someone they can respect as an educator, someone that they can look up to?"[12.6]

While there's some ambiguity about when (or even if) Deweese was fired—the DISD refused to comment, saying it was a personnel matter—it's pretty apparent that her teaching career ended sometime around October 10, 2013.[127] According to Deweese's Twitter feed (@CristyNicoleMDL), she reactivated her profile page on ModelMayhem.com that same afternoon, and the following day, tweeted that she was unable to comment:

> Thank you everyone for the support. I am unable to make comments at this moment but I'd like you all to know that I appreciate the love!— Cristy Nicole (@CristyNicoleMDL) October 11, 2013

A lot of that love came from students (both male and female) at the school, who launched a [now-defunct] Facebook page, "Support Teacher Cristy Nicole Deweese," signed petitions on her behalf, tweeted supportive posts and photos, and even launched a sign campaign in the school to promote the hashtag #SaveMsDeweese. None of this made any difference in Deweese's case, but it does raise the possibility that societal attitudes towards this type of online activity may slowly change in the future, particularly given the stunningly large number of people who have taken and shared their own nude photos over the past decade, and the fact that younger people have less problem with online nudity. In fact, it apparently didn't occur to Deweese that her photo shoot might be problem; she actually talks about her plans to become a Spanish teacher in her video trailer for Playboy.com.

But what about teachers who have starred in adult films? Will they (or should they) ever be able to work as educators? Most of the examples I've uncovered in my research make it seem pretty unlikely; administrators generally waste no time in firing someone who qualifies for an entry in the Internet Adult Film Database. A good example of how long-lasting the prohibition can be arose in Paducah, KY in 2006, when a student recognized his Reidland High School science teacher, Tericka Dye, on the cover of an adult video. When the principal heard that the video was being shared among students (and some parents), he called Dye to his office to ask about her participation in the video and when she confirmed it, immediately suspended her. Dye admitted to school officials that she started performing under the name "Rikki Andersin" (or Anderson) when she was 22, homeless, and desperate for work. She reportedly appeared in 11 adult films between 1997 and 1999, and then left the adult industry. Despite her positive teaching reviews and support from members of the community, her contract was terminated.

As Dye later told talk host Dr. Phil Ozman in a nationally-televised interview, "I just don't understand how you can take a teacher who has put so much into it, and suspend them for something that is 11 years in the past. I did live with the fear that somehow, someday, it would catch up with me. I just didn't know that it would ruin me."[12.8]

Dye re-applied for her position in Paducah, but when she was turned down, she filed suit against the District seeking damages and reinstatement. During her appeal of a lower court's dismissal, Dye agreed to withdraw her suit in exchange for a clean employment record. She then changed her name to Tera Myer, and after applying for positions in several states, landed a job at the Parkway North High School in St. Louis.[12.9]

Just four years later, Myer found herself in precisely the same situation. After one of her students at Parkway North High found photos and information about her adult film work online, she met with the school administration and agreed not to finish out the school year. When questioned about how Myer had been hired despite her adult film career, a district representative said that a call had been placed to the Paducah district but officials there did not explain why Myer had left.[12.10]

Since there are far more women who work in adult films and a much larger number of female teachers, relatively few men lose their jobs in precisely this fashion, but it does happen. In the summer of 2012, it was discovered that Massachusetts teacher Kevin Hogan, the chair of the English department at the Mystic Valley Regional Charter School, had made three gay-themed adult films in 2010 under the screen name "Hytch Cawke."[12.11] Six months later, after repeated inquires by Boston's Fox25, the station that broke the story, Mystic Valley confirmed that Hogan was no longer employed at the school.[12.12]

There may be some small signs, however, that the climate for teachers with adult industry film experience may be changing. In 2011, substitute teacher Shawn Loftis was called one morning and told not to come to work at the Nautilus Middle School in Miami Beach after administrators there learned that not only had he starred in adult films for three or four years under the name "Collin O'Neal" but had actually operated his own adult film company. After a brief investigation, he was terminated for violating a provision of the Miami-Dade school district contract, which reads: "[Teachers] are expected to conduct themselves both in their employment and in the community in a manner that will reflect credit upon themselves and the school system."[12,13]

After subsequently losing his state teaching license, Loftis appealed to the Florida Education Practices Commission, and in a somewhat surprising decision, the Commission reinstated him. Among other things, the Commission said that his work in the adult film industry was not illegal and that as a result, the school lacked authority to terminate his contract on that basis. However, the Commission did impose a two-year probationary period.[12,14]

Let's be perfectly clear, however: that fact that the Florida Education Practices Commission ruled that Loftis's school should not have fired him is not the same thing as saying that it should hire him back, or that another school should offer him a contract. As Miami-Dade Schools spokesman John Schuster pointed out in an interview, "Having a teaching certificate is not a guarantee of employment as a teacher. School districts are under no obligation to provide employment to any individual just because they hold a teaching certificate." Loftis told reporters that if Miami-Dade Schools refused to reinstate him, "They're going to have a lawsuit on their fucking hands. They should expect a discrimination suit that will be played out on television."[12.15] It's unclear, however, whether Loftis actually carried through on his threat.

Even if a school district might be inclined to give Loftis an opportunity to teach (and realistically, given the competition for teaching jobs these days, it would be so much easier to simply not bother), the chances of a district offering a job to a currently-active adult film star are essentially zero. That's the challenge facing Florida fishing charter model Tiffany Shepherd. In the aftermath to her firing, Shepherd reportedly received numerous offers to pose nude and semi-nude from various adult magazines, including *Playboy*, but turned them all down because she hoped to find a new teaching position.[12.16]

However, despite reportedly sending out 2,500 resumes, Shepherd was unable to find a new teaching position. Increasingly desperate for work, she decided to take the somewhat dubious advice of Captain Gil Coombes, who not only ran Smokin' Em Charters, but also operated an adult webcam site with his wife Kat. According to published reports, Coombes told Shepherd that she would never work as a teacher again, and that she should capitalize on her new-found fame by making adult films. Shepherd adopted the screen name "Leah Lust," and made at least five adult films, including one called *My First Sex Teacher*.[12.17] It's a little unclear as to whether Shepherd/Lust is still active in adult films, although the *Palm Beach Post* recent published a photo gallery that suggests that she is still is.[12.18]

"I'm not particularly proud of [my adult film career]. To be honest, I hate it," Shepherd told one media outlet. "I'm an educated woman, but I never thought it would come to this. No one gets brought up thinking they'll be a floozy."[12.19] Words to the wise.

~~~~~~~~~~

Chapter Thirteen
Prostitution

The "most ancient profession in the world," as Rudyard Kipling once famously described prostitution, has enthusiastically adopted the technological tools of the 21st century.[13.1] Thanks to the ubiquitous availability of sites for advertising escort services, prostitutes are now just a click away for clients willing to risk criminal prosecution, sexually transmitted diseases, and worse. Escorts can run inexpensive classified ads in online services, and there are even a growing number of Web sites and online forums on which patrons review the escorts they've hired.

On the flip side, the Internet is making it safer and more efficient for police departments to combat the prostitution trade. Police, of course, have been catching patrons of prostitutes for decades, if not centuries. While departments still send out female officers as decoys on sketchy urban streets, the most effective method these days is to place a provocative ad in exactly the same online sites that prostitutes and escorts themselves use. If interested customers respond, they're given instructions on where to meet. Once money is offered for sex, the party comes to a crashing halt. To add a final digital indignity to the proceedings, an increasing number of police departments are posting mug shots of the johns they arrest to police department Web sites in an effort to use "Internet shaming" to help combat the prostitution trade.

The individuals snared in these online prostitution stings come from a broad swath of society, and teachers, unfortunately, are not exempt. Every few weeks, reports emerge of another teacher caught up in an anti-prostitution sweep somewhere around the United States.

One of the more disturbing aspects of these cases is that so many of the ads that seem to snare teachers (and others) either implicitly or explicitly state that the person posting the ad is under the age of 18. For instance, in March 2014, a high school chemistry teacher in Phoenix, AZ named Jerry Marfe responded to an online ad purportedly offering "adult services" from a pair of high school cheerleader prostitutes. Police used a hidden camera to record Marfe's conversation with the female decoy, who told Marfe that she was 16 and asked if he was a teacher. After being arrested for offering money to have sex with the "prostitute," Marfe was immediately placed on leave by the administration at Betty H. Fairfax High School, and resigned a few days later. In mid-June, Marfe was sentenced to 15 days in prison and 10 years of supervised release.[13,2]

Similarly, police in Winona County, Minnesota ran an online ad that "displayed a girl wearing minimal clothing, in sexually suggestive positions. It also included language commonly used in ads that is consistent with minors advertising sex acts for money." Police said that they started getting hits on the ads within minutes of its going live.

Among the people who made arrangements to meet with a "15-year-old girl" was Bret Emmel, a retired health teacher at the Longellow Middle School in the Lacrosse School District. The district promptly told Emmel that his coaching and substitute teaching services were no longer required.[13.3]

Teachers are not only caught soliciting prostitutes, they are also arrested for offering to provide such services. Down in Texas in 2008, Cleveland High School drama teacher and student council advisor Laurie Ann Lewis struck up a conversation with a man in an online chat room and offered to meet him as an escort at the Four Seasons Hotel in downtown Houston. After she offered to perform a sexual act for $300, she was arrested and charged with prostitution.[13.4] Before the school board could vote to terminate her contract, Lewis resigned from the Cleveland Independent School District on August 19, 2008.[13.5] When a reporter asked Rhonda Perrin, Lewis's next-door neighbor, to describe her, she replied: "She looks like your typical soccer mom. She's a very nice, quiet neighbor. It makes me wonder if we ought to pay our teachers more."[13.6]

Given the position that teachers hold in society, it shouldn't come as a surprise that busted educators are usually featured prominently in any headline and/or article discussing a prostitution bust. Moreover, given the heightened moral standard to which educators are held, no teacher or administrator should reasonably expect to still be teaching if (or more likely, when) the news breaks that they've been strolling down the dark side of the Information Highway.

That's particularly true if teachers are caught using school equipment to find escorts. A couple of years ago, the name of Brantley High School chemistry teacher Christopher Dalland turned up on a list of brothel clients in East Orange County, Florida. He was placed on administrative leave and resigned rather than face firing by the school board.[13.7] A subsequent investigation by the high school revealed that Dalland had been using his school-issued computer to troll escort Web sites. The district revealed that Dalland had been reprimanded for similar activity in 2007, but had successfully completed a two-year probation.[13.8]

Another egregious cybertrap that some teachers have managed to fall into is using a school computer to set up meetings with prostitution clients. On February 10, 2009, 32-year-old Amber Carter, a fourth-grade teacher at the Western Elementary School in the Bellefontaine City School District in Ohio, told her principal she was taking a half-day of sick leave. A short time later, the principal was shocked to learn that Carter had been busted for prostitution by the sheriff's department in a sex sting at a Super 8 Motel just two miles from Western Elementary.[13.9]

According to reports subsequently filed by the local sheriff's office, detectives received an anonymous email tip on February 4 that Carter was offering sexual services for cash on Craigslist. An undercover detective responded to the advertisement and over the next several days, exchanged twenty-four emails with Carter in which they negotiated time, place, and price; several of the emails were sent by Carter during school hours. After Carter was arrested, detectives from the sheriff's office went to Western Elementary and seized her computer for forensic analysis. Carter was immediately placed on administrative leave, but said that she would not resign.[13.10] Just over a week later, however, Carter changed her mind and submitted her resignation;[13.11] in early March 2009, she pleaded guilty to solicitation and was given two years' probation and a suspended 30-day jail sentence.[13.12]

Sometimes, it takes the district a little time to find out that prostitution has been taking place. In 2010, Solona Islam, a math teacher at McClellan Magnet High School in Little Rock, plead guilty to a misdemeanor prostitution charge. Islam (who was the 2002 valedictorian for McClellan High) told a reporter that she was desperate for money, and thought that she would just be working for a dating service, not an escort site.[13.13]

"When you look at your check and it's only $600 and you know your rent is $700, and the light bill is coming up and your child needs day care paid. It was a point of desperation." she said. "I decided at the tail end of it when he offered the sex for extra money to do it."[13.14]

Because Islam plead guilty to a misdemeanor, police were not required to contact district officials, and Islam did not tell them either, arguing that the school had no business knowing about her personal affairs. After a reporter tipped them off about Islam's plea, however, she was suspended and placed on paid administrative leave. She resigned on February 18,

2011, but worried about how future employers might view her. "I am a human," Islam told a reporter. "They can't see a teacher beyond seeing this is a perfect role model and be perfect all the time."[13,15]

As with other types of cybertraps, the question arises as to whether any involvement with prostitution is a permanent bar against teaching again at some point. That's a question that confronted Melissa Petro, an elementary school art teacher in the Bronx after she published an essay on HuffingtonPost.com in which she admitted accepting money for sex from men she met on Craigslist.

From October 2006 to January 2007 I accepted money in exchange for sexual services I provided to men I met online in what was then called the "erotic services" section of Craigslist.org. ... At Craigslist.org, I was able to bill myself as exactly what I was at the time: a graduate student, bored and curious, sexually uninhibited, looking to make a little money while having a little fun. I wrote my own ads, screened my own prospective dates, decided on my own what I would and would not do for money, and—best of all—I kept every penny I earned, all without the interference of an agency or other ubiquitous "middle man."

Ultimately, while my experience as a "non-pro" was not the "fun" I had come looking for—I found the lifestyle physically demanding, emotionally taxing and spiritually bankrupting, and so I made a decision to desist some months after I'd gotten started, exiting the industry just as freely as I'd entered—never have I felt it was the state's obligation—nor its right, in fact—to protect me from the decisions I made.[13.16]

Not surprisingly, the fallout from Petro's column was rapid. She was placed on administrative leave by the New York City Department of Education, and assigned to a so-called "rubber room" in downtown Brooklyn. The following spring, her contract was terminated and she agreed not to look for work in the New York school system again.[13.17] At a subsequent press conference with her attorney Gloria Allred, Petro explained her decision not to pursue a lawsuit against the Department of Education:

It was my belief that the First Amendment protected my right to publish my experiences and opinions—however controversial. Although I could have fought my removal I have decided, instead, to move on. Regardless of the outcome of a trial, which I have every reason to believe I would have won, I do not believe I would have ever been welcomed back to the classroom by the Department of Education.[13.18]

Whether you agree with Petro's termination or not, she is correct. In our society, we've given second chances to any number of people—U.S. Senators and Presidents, bankers, lawyers, NFL quarterbacks, to name just a few—who have experienced ethical lapses or even committed actual, serious crimes. But we hold teachers to a nearly flawless standard of moral perfection, and demonstrate a cold and abrupt disdain for any perceived flaws.

Although such high standards may be eroded by the digital age in the years to come, in the interim, current and prospective teachers need to be aware of the ever-growing reach of the Internet into every aspect of our lives, and make conscious choices accordingly.

~~~~~~~~

Section III
Cybertraps Involving Students

"I think I'm going to like school here," [Anne Shirley] announced. "I don't think much of the master, though. He's all the time curling his mustache and making eyes at Prissy Andrews. Prissy is grown up, you know. She's sixteen and she's studying for the entrance examination into Queen's Academy at Charlottetown next year. Tillie Boulter says the master is DEAD GONE on her. She's got a beautiful complexion and curly brown hair and she does it up so elegantly. She sits in the long seat at the back and he sits there, too, most of the time—to explain her lessons, he says. But Ruby Gillis says she saw him writing something on her slate and when Prissy read it she blushed as red as a beet and giggled; and Ruby Gillis says she doesn't believe it had anything to do with the lesson."—L.M. Montgomery, *Anne of Green Gables*, Chapter XV.

Although this is a book about the myriad changes wrought by technology and the numerous cybertraps that have arisen or have been exacerbated, it is worth remembering that inappropriate relationships between teachers and students have been around pretty much since the start of schooling. Nonetheless, there is no question that digital technology has profoundly altered the relationship between educators and students. On the one hand, it has made students more accessible and vulnerable to teachers, and has lowered the barriers to inappropriate behavior; voyeurism and sexual solicitation are now just a click of a button away. At the same time, technology also has brought its relentless leveling effect to the classroom: It is now far easier for students to inflict serious, even career-ending harm on a disliked teacher, again with little more than the push of a few buttons. As my teacher friends have told me repeatedly, this makes an already difficult job that much harder.

Given how new all of this technology is (we're just two decades into the World Wide Web, and less than a decade into the smartphone era), it's not surprising that we don't have well-developed social norms and district procedures around electronic behavior. These will develop and become ingrained over time; in the interim, teachers need to educate themselves about the potential relationship cybertraps that can ensnare them and their students, and encourage their schools to develop and implement digital citizenship curricula for students in every grade level.

~~~~~~~~~

Chapter Fourteen
Cyberbullying and Cyberbaiting

The issue of cyberbullying among students has gotten a lot of attention over the past decade, particularly as the percentage of children using mobile devices has more than tripled since 2004. Increasingly, cyberbullying is identified as a severely disruptive threat to the school environment, one that poses a significant risk to the mental and physical health of the children involved. Only recently, however, have people begun to focus on the fact that teachers are often the ones being bullied by both students and their parents.

As with so many of the other issues discussed in this book, the underlying behavior is not a new phenomenon. Students have been playing pranks on teachers for a long, long time: crickets in the ceiling, frogs in desk drawers, tacks on the seat, and so on. However, those were localized events, and easily dealt with, none of them, in today's vernacular, "went viral." Today's technology has not only changed the nature of the pranks that kids can play, it also has dramatically expanded the potential audience. Kids no longer harass teachers for the sake of few moments of laughter from their classmates; they are now competing to see how many hits or likes they can get on YouTube, Facebook, Instagram, and the like.

Cyberbullying

There is little disputing the fact that digital abuse of teachers is a growing problem. A 2006 survey by the National School Boards Association found that 26% of teachers in the U.S. had been targeted by cyberbullying.[14.1] In 2011, a survey of United Kingdom teachers by Plymouth University found that 35 percent of respondents had experienced some kind cyberbullying. Teachers reported that 72 percent of the bullying was done by students and 26 percent by parents.[14.2] A more recent UK study by the National Association of Schoolmasters Union of Women Teachers found a lower rate of cyberbullying (roughly 21%), but the bullying was arguably more derogatory and involved a wider age range of children (including some as young as 4–7 years of age).[14.3]

The tools used to cyberbully teachers will be familiar to anyone who has studied the issue of cyberbullying among students. That makes sense, of course; students are generally adept at using technology, and can turn it to whatever ends best serve their purpose at the moment. Teachers report that they have been bullied via text messages, on social media posts (particularly Facebook, Twitter, and Instagram), in chat rooms and other online fora, on Web sites like RateMyTeachers.com or even on student-created Web sites targeted at embarrassing or libeling a specific teacher. The surveyed UK students reported that 47 percent of the online comments consisted of assorted insults and 50 percent were derogatory assessments of their performance; over one-quarter of the comments included photos or videos that were taken without the consent of the targeted teacher.[144]

Many of these online attacks come within the scope of general anti-cyberbullying statutes, but the problem has grown sufficiently serious that the North Carolina legislature recently adopted a law (arguably unconstitutional) that imposes up to a month-long jail sentence and/or a $1,000 fine on any 15–17-year-old who "intimidate[s] or threaten[s]" a teacher.[145] Of course, given the fact that UK researchers found that the "vast majority" of the online bullying of teachers was committed by students 11–16, it's not clear that the North Carolina law will have the preventative effect that the legislators hope.[146]

One of the interesting questions is whether a specific law against bullying teachers will encourage more teachers to report abuse. It is discouraging but not surprising to note that nearly 60 percent of the teachers who admitted to being bullied did not bother to report the abuse to their administrators or, presumably, to the online services involved. Much of the reluctance can be attributed to the sheer difficulty of identifying the perpetrators; it is far too easy for online bullies to hide their identity, at least on a superficial level.[147] Disturbingly, some teachers also report a reluctance to report online bullying due to fear that the allegations will result in discipline by skittish administrators more concerned about potential liability than conducting a fair investigation. That being said, things have progressed from the early days of the World Wide Web, when administrators and school boards had a much harder time believing that students were capable of using Internet tools to malign their teachers. Few have any remaining illusions on that score.

Cyberbaiting

If people have any lingering doubts regarding the vulnerability of teachers and the sometimes vicious nature of children, they need look no further than YouTube. In the past few years, smartphones, YouTube, and adolescent mischief have brewed together into a toxic mix we now call "cyberbaiting."

The Urban Dictionary defines "cyberbaiting" as follows:

> [W]hen students, either individually or as a group, make a plan to act so outrageously that the classroom teacher loses self control and begins yelling or acting in another unprofessional manner. The teacher is surreptitiously recorded, and the video of the momentary loss of control is posted to social networking sites.[14.8]

A brief search on YouTube illustrates the scope of the problem. Type in the keywords "teacher loses it" and you'll get a long list of disturbing titles. Examples include:

- "Arundel Middle School Teacher Loses It";
- "Teacher Flipping Out Throws Stuff in Classroom";
- "Teacher loses it when kid texts in class";

- "Teacher Loses It in School"; and
- "Teacher Loses It with a Mental Meltdown".

The 2011 edition of the *Norton Online Family Report* found that over 20% of teachers had either been a victim of cyberbaiting or knew a colleague who had been.[14.9] Not all of the examples in the list above are actual cyberbaiting, but they do help to underscore the extent to which teachers should assume they are always on camera. A study conducted of 18-year-olds that same year by Bridgewater State University's Massachusetts Aggression Reduction Center found that over 20 percent of boys and 13 percent of girls took photos and videos of teachers without permission and just 2.3 percent were caught doing so.[14.10]

The Center's director, Dr. Elizabeth Englander, told ABC News that the real problem lies in the education (and implicitly, the parenting) of smartphone-equipped children. "The real problem," she said, "is that we are not teaching our children how to think about and to control the use of technology. We are just giving them extra powerful technology and not discussing it with them. It's like back in 1928, when you got a driver's license just because you bought a car."[14.11]

Dr. Englander is exactly right. While it is not realistic to think that we can completely stamp out bullying behavior by children, either towards their peers or their teachers, we can make significant progress if we develop and implement effective K-12 curricula, and encourage school administrators and parents to hold their children responsible for online misbehavior.

~~~~~~~~~

Chapter Fifteen
The Perils of Fake Social Media Accounts

On July 5, 1993, the *New Yorker* published what would become the most-reproduced cartoon in its long and storied history: Peter Steiner's iconic drawing of two canines at a computer, with the prescient caption, "On the Internet, nobody knows you're a dog."[15.1] It was a remarkable insight, coming as it did 13 years before Facebook and Twitter, and 17 years before Instagram. But Steiner deftly identified the central dilemma of the information highway: no driver's licenses that help us identify who is actually at the wheel (or keyboard).

True anonymity on the Internet is actually an elusive thing. Every device that connects to the Internet is assigned a unique **Internet Protocol** ("IP") address that makes it possible for information to be sent from Internet servers to that particular device. But it also makes it possible for law enforcement (and music labels and movie studios) to identify people who commit criminal acts online or steal content. The vast majority of IP addresses are managed by Internet Service Providers, who assign them to specific subscribers. The ISP maintains records of which IP addresses are assigned to each subscriber, and may also track when, how long, and for what purpose the IP address was used. An investigator armed with a subpoena (or a National Security Letter) can obtain that information and link it to a physical address, which then makes it possible to obtain a search warrant. All too often, the first indication a parent has that their precocious 9th-grader has been hacking into the school computer or has set up a fake Facebook account to mock a teacher is when the police show up with a search warrant to examine all the digital devices in the household. (Teachers, unfortunately, are often similarly surprised.)

Kids were remarkably quick to see the harassing potential of social media services. In 2006, for instance, when the social media site Myspace was less than 3 years old, a number of Sarasota County students were disciplined for using the site to harass their teachers. One North Port High School student (who was sued by his victim) created a fake Myspace page that suggested the teacher hated her students and hoped that they would all die. He also uploaded a photo of the teacher and captioned it with sexually explicit comments. Several of his classmates chimed in with their own inappropriate comments.[15.2] At almost exactly the same time, halfway across the country, a Minnesota 8th grader was identified as the creator of a fake Myspace page that was intended to create the impression that his Coon Rapids Middle School English teacher was a child pornographer. The profile was set up in the teacher's name and contained a variety of links to child pornography. With the help of some classmates and an 11th-grader at the Coon Rapids high school, the boy set up another profile on which the teacher "said" that he liked to molest female students and tell anti-Semitic jokes. The student was identified when classmates told the principal that they had heard him boasting about the pages.[15.3]

Recognizing the problem, Facebook early on decided that it would require people to use "real names" when they created user accounts. According to Chris Cox, Facebook's vice-president of product, the goal was to make sure that people were using "authentic" names:

> We believe this is the right policy for Facebook for two reasons. First, it's part of what made Facebook special in the first place, by differentiating the service from the rest of the Internet where pseudonymity, anonymity, or often random names were the social norm. Second, it's the primary mechanism we have to protect millions of people every day, all around the world, from real harm. The stories of mass impersonation, trolling, domestic abuse, and higher rates of bullying and intolerance are oftentimes the result of people hiding behind fake names, and it's both terrifying and sad. Our ability to successfully protect against them with this policy has borne out the reality that this policy, on balance, and when applied carefully, is a very powerful force for good.[15.4]

Facebook's efforts to prevent fake accounts have not been overwhelmingly successful, and this problem has contributed to the serious shift that has occurred in teacher-student relationships. In the eight years since Facebook became generally available, students have been caught setting up fake Facebook pages to bully classmates, harass teachers, and advocate for various dubious causes. One typical example occurred on Prince Edward Island in 2011, when a student at East Wiltshire Intermediate School in Cornwall created a Facebook account in a teacher's name. As the CBC put it, with typical Canadian understatement, the student then filled the account "with false information about the teacher's interests and views."[15.5]

One question that frequently arises is whether the First Amendment protects a student' use of Facebook. For instance, if a student creates a Facebook group called "Ms. Sarah Phelps is the worst teacher I've ever met!," is that cyberbullying of a teacher, or is it legitimate free speech? That was the issue raised by Katherine Evans, a student at Pembroke Pines Student High School, who created the group and invited her classmates to "express your feelings of hatred." Evans was suspended for three days and took the group down, but later filed a lawsuit against the school principal alleging a violation of her First Amendment rights.[15.6] After a federal magistrate ruled that her Facebook group was protected off-campus speech, Evans eventually settled her suit for $15,000 in lawyer's fees, and $1 in damages.[15.7] An important point is that even though Evans's page was unkind, she wasn't attempting to impersonate her teacher.

A related issue is whether parents should be liable if their child creates a fake Facebook page to cyberbully another student (or a teacher). In October 2014, the Georgia Court of Appeals ruled that parents could be held liable for the actions of their minor child if they learn of the bullying page and fail to take it down. The Court clearly stated that liability does not arise automatically out of the parent-child relationship, but only if it can be shown that the parents themselves were negligent.[15.8] Presumably, the same logic would apply if the child had targeted a teacher instead of another child.

Educators seem to be less likely to use fake Facebook or other social media accounts to bully students (although, as we'll see, they do use them for more salacious purposes). Where educators have stumbled, however, is in using social media to surreptitiously monitor student activity. In 2012, it was discovered that Louise Losos, the principal of Clayton High School in Clayton, Missouri, was using a fake Facebook profile to "friend" students and parents so that she could monitor posts, photos, and comments. Her cover was blown when a graduating senior, Chase Haslett, posted a message to a school-related page that read: "Whoever is friends with Suzy Harriston on Facebook needs to drop them. It is the Clayton Principal." The "Suzy Harriston" profile was quickly deleted, and the district announced that Losos would take a personal leave of absence for the remainder of the year, citing a "fundamental dispute concerning the appropriate use of social media." Losos subsequently resigned her position.[15.9]

Not surprisingly, there are some school districts that are more comfortable than others with the idea of using fake Facebook accounts to monitor student behavior. One common approach is to outsource the surveillance to a student resource officer from the local police department (which raises its own issues of propriety and setting positive examples for students). For instance, in South Burlington, Vermont, nearly two dozen lacrosse players were disciplined in early 2008 after the school's SRO saw numerous Facebook photos showing underage alcohol consumption. The SRO, Cpl. Tonya Lawyer, told a local reporter that she and other officers routinely created fake social media profiles for investigative purposes.

"We go on, we make up fake IDs, fake names, and we hope to get invited in," Cpl. Lawyer said. "Once I've linked myself to one South Burlington kid, I can usually get linked to other South Burlington kids."[15.10]

On those social media services that don't even make a nod to identity accountability (such as Twitter or Instagram), or which actively encourage anonymity (including apps such as Whisper and Secret), bullying is far too easy. On Twitter, for instance, students can set up anonymous accounts to use for targeting victims, or as with Facebook, set up accounts that purport to be the property of the victim.

In the strictest interpretation of events, students who engage in that type of behavior are committing the crime of identity theft. It may be that the intention is fairly harmless and no more serious than sticking a frog in a teacher's handbag. But for a variety of reasons, kids are less innocent today, and far too often think that it is hysterically funny to impute racist behavior or sexual misconduct to their teachers. A typical example: At Lawrence High School in Lawrence, IN, kids created Twitter accounts for various teachers during the 2011-12 school year, and then sent out tweets that suggested, among other things, that the white football coach only wanted black players on his team, that the wrestling coach was having sex with his athletes, and that the basketball coach kept a careful eye on high school girls in black yoga pants.[15,11]

This insidious practice of falsely attributing embarrassing or even criminal statements to someone is known as "cyberbullying by proxy," and it is very difficult to combat, particularly given the enthusiasm of many social media services for anonymity. Fortunately, school boards and school districts are more aware of the potential problem these days and less likely to react in a knee-jerk fashion whenever it looks like a teacher has said something inappropriate online. There is a serious debate to be had about the importance of anonymity for adults, but I think that a compelling case can be made that among children, the problems created by easy anonymity online greatly outweigh the potential benefits.

In the meantime, embrace the Socratic wisdom that "The un-Googled life is not worth living." The practical reality is that it is not possible to prevent bored, mischievous, or malicious students from misusing technology, so it is important to regularly search the Web to see what someone might have posted about you. Each of us, ultimately, is responsible for curating and protecting our digital brand. The sooner you become aware of a potential problem, the easier it is to deal with it.

~~~~~~~~~

Chapter Sixteen
Cyberharassment and Cyberstalking

Cyberharassment and cyberstalking are two variants on the concept of cyberbullying, but with an added component of obsession that typically goes beyond the more ephemeral and often temporary nature of cyberbullying. As we'll see, educators can be both victims and perpetrators of these offenses.

Cyberharassment

Cyberbullying and cyberharassment are often lumped together in single state statute, or a state will have a prohibition against one type of electronic misbehavior and not the other. According to the National Conference of State Legislatures, "cyberharassment" is typically defined as "threatening or harassing email messages, instant messages, or blog entries or websites dedicated solely to tormenting an individual."[16.1] In those states that do not have a separate cyberharassment statute, it is common for prosecutors to rely on the more general harassment statute to cover acts involving social media and other types of electronic communication.

For instance, in the summer of 2013, a math teacher at Timber Creek High School in Gloucester Township named David A. Clune was charged with harassing two recent female graduates, one aged 17 and the other 18. Police said that Clune sent over 70 text and Facebook messages to the two students; an arbitrator later ruled that the messages "clearly rise to the level of solicitation ..." and upheld his firing by the school district.[16.2]

What is particularly disturbing is the ease with which virtually any online resource or social media service can be used for bullying and harassment. The Web site Ask.fm, for instance, is notorious among child safety advocates for its frequent appearances in teen cyberbullying cases. Not long ago, a Connecticut teacher allegedly got the same idea. Stephanie DeFrance, a well-regarded teacher (and former "Teacher of the Year") at the Totoket Valley Elementary School in North Branford, CT, was charged in May 2014 with using the Web site to harass a 15-year-old girl. DeFrance was reportedly angry that the victim was involved with her daughter's boyfriend, and used Ask.fm to send her over 65 hostile messages over a 90-day stretch.[16.3] DeFrance pleaded not guilty to the charges in May 2014.[16.4]

Teachers, of course, can just as easily become victims of harassment as students, particularly as new and unfamiliar apps or social media services emerge. In the spring of 2014, for instance, an app called "Streetchat" was released; according to the app's own description,

Streetchat is an anonymous bulletin board to post photos to the people in your school. It is a fast reliable way to share your thoughts and talk about things around you.

In October, however, Norwalk police arrested a 14-year-old student and charged him or her (details were not released) with using Streetchat to post photos of a Spanish teacher with captions that suggested that she was engaging in "unprofessional relations" with her students. When law enforcement examined the teen's phone, they found a variety of other images intended to cyberbully others at the school. The ease with which Streetchat can be used for cyberbullying and cyberharassment has alarmed educators and law enforcement, and inspired some teens to campaign for school-wide bans of the app.[16.5]

It's important to remember that many of the other activities described in this book, including fake Web pages, cyberbaiting, and so forth, can serve as the basis for a charge of cyberharassment. It is not uncommon for a harasser to use multiple modes of communication to abuse his or her victim.

Cyberstalking

"Cyberstalking" is defined by the National Conference of State Legislatures as "the use of the Internet, email or other electronic communications to stalk someone, and generally refers to a pattern of threatening or malicious behaviors … posing a credible threat of physical harm."[16.6] The credible threat may consist of an explicit statement, or may simply stem from the pattern of behavior. Whether a pattern of behavior rises to the level of cyberstalking or is "merely" cyberharassment typically depends on the facts of the case and the specific language of the state statute in question.

In some jurisdictions, the line between cyberharassment and cyberstalking is a little blurry. For instance, North Carolina defines cyberstalking in part as "[e]lectronically mail or electronically communicate to another and to knowingly make any false statement concerning death, injury, illness, disfigurement, indecent conduct, or criminal conduct of the person electronically mailed or of any member of the person's family or household with the intent to abuse, annoy, threaten, terrify, harass, or embarrass."[16.7] In 2008, a freshman at Providence High School in South Charlotte set up a Web site accusing one of his teachers of being a pedophile. The site contained an online message board with derogatory comments, a link to a fake Web site called "teacherpedofiles.com" with the teacher's name on it, and a bunch of photos taken surreptitiously during class. He was charged with cyberstalking under the North Carolina statute.[16.8]

In the majority of cyberstalking cases, however, the physical threat to the potential victim is clear, or the online conduct is so abusive (even in the absence of a specific threat) that the victim is terrified. A typical example: Megan Mantooth, a 26-year-old eighth-grade teacher at the Burgaw Middle School in Burgaw, NC, was charged in 2011 with cyberstalking a 13-year-old boy after sending him hundreds of text messages, many of which contained sexual innuendo. Among other things, she told the boy that she would "look better in a bikini" than his middle school classmates.[16.9]

Mantooth's cyberstalking came to light when the boy turned the phone over to his parents, who continued the text conversation with his teacher for a brief time before turning the phone over to local law enforcement. A month later, she accepted a plea deal that postponed her trial for three years with the proviso that if she adhered to the conditions of probation, the case would be dismissed. In a written letter to the boy and his family, Mantooth acknowledge her mistake:

I am deeply, terribly sorry for the pain and anguish I have caused. I myself am in complete and total shock that this situation went as far as it did. I knew better than to do what I was doing. There are no excuses for my actions, and I sincerely regret them. I apologize to everyone involved in the situation. I promise that I will never do anything like this again. I am deeply ashamed of what has happened - I knew lines had been crossed and said things that should never have been said. I implore you for your forgiveness.[16.10]

Notwithstanding the plea deal and her apology, Mantooth's teaching license was revoked by the State of North Carolina a year later.[16.11]

Another example of a teacher cyberstalking a student occurred in western Pennsylvania in the summer of 2014. Michael David Garet, a Spanish teacher at Penn-Trafford High School in Harrison City, PA, was suspended after being charged with stalking, harassment, and disorderly conduct.

Police allege that Garet started messaging a male student on Google+, and then on other social media channels, including Facebook and Twitter. He repeatedly invited the student to spend time alone with him or go on trips, and then began trying to set up meetings with the boy at his workplace.[16.12]

The school district was praised by law enforcement for its swift response to the situation. The boy's mother reported the situation to another teacher in the school on January 31, 2014, and the teacher promptly told the school principal. Garet was suspended without pay and escorted off the campus by police on the morning of February 4. As District Superintendent Matt Harris told reporters, "You don't take chances, and you turn over everything."[16.13]

Harris's words should be a mantra for every school district administrator. Some of the most disturbing cases of student harassment (or even assault) involve teachers who get into trouble in one district, are told to leave, and then commit similar offenses in the new district. Some school districts are all too willing to engage in the process of "passing the trash" in an effort to minimize the harm to their students and avoid possible litigation with the disgraced teacher. Other institutions—notably the Catholic Church—have engaged in similar practices. No child down the road should suffer preventable harm; every school district should promptly and honestly disclose when any educator is released or disciplined for harassing or assaulting a student.

~~~~~~~~~

Chapter Seventeen
Digital Voyeurism and the Production of Child Pornography

Don't Be a Digital Voyeur

The first of these two cybertraps refers to the process of surreptitiously taking electronic images and recordings of someone for prurient purposes. Thanks in large part to the fast-paced evolution of technology, it has gotten easier and easier to hide digital cameras in a wide variety of inappropriate place, which has proven to be a dangerous temptation for numerous educators (and a wide variety of other professionals as well). Among the hidden camera-related voyeurism offenses for which educators have been arrested are: taking upskirt photos during music lessons,[17.1] hiding a camera in packet of hotel coffee to secretly videotape a student showering,[17.2] hiding a camera in a theater dressing room,[17.3] and putting a digital camera in a bottle of shampoo to secretly record both faculty and students in a locker room shower.[17.4] That is, unfortunately, just a small sampling of the disturbing uses to which tiny cameras have been put.

In the majority of digital voyeurism cases, the images and videos are intended for the private consumption of the person who took them. Unfortunately, however, it is far too easy for any digital content to be shared with the rest of the world, and there is unquestionably a thriving market for surreptitious images of schoolchildren. A typical example of this type of crime occurred fairly early in the Web era in Greenwich, Connecticut, in 2001. Parents of cheerleaders at the Greenwich Academy were horrified to discover that a Web site, cheervideos.com, featured unauthorized videos of their daughters. Even more upsetting was the fact that the videos repeatedly zoomed up the skirts or down the blouses of the teenage girls. The site was owned and operated by Kevin Dern, a music teacher at the Academy, who was charged with more than 50 counts of child pornography and civil rights violations. The investigation subsequently revealed that Dern had more than 9,000 child pornography images on his computer, which led to further criminal charges.[17.5]

As is so often the case, the Internet has taken what was once a relatively limited phenomenon and institutionalized it. In 2005, a pair of University of Virginia roommates created a site called "Reddit," which allows users to post links, text, and photos for other users to vote up or down. The most highly-rated posts are displayed on Reddit's main page, which the founders grandly proclaimed to be "the front page of the Internet." The site also allows users to create pages, known as "subreddits," that focus on specific topics. Not surprisingly, many of the subreddits involve various sexual themes.

In 2012, some students at East Coweta High School in Coweta County, Georgia discovered that photos of them, taken during the school day, had been posted to a subreddit called "Creepshots." Although the subreddit has since been banned by Reddit, the description and "rules" of the subreddit are still available online. The text offers some chilling insights into the attitudes that underlie so much misogynistic activity on the Internet:

Welcome to CreepShots

Thank you for visiting our subreddit. Now that you are here, the first question in your mind may very well be **'What is a CreepShot?'**
Creepshots are *CANDID*. If a person is posing for and/or aware that a picture is being taken, then it ceases to be candid and thus is no longer a creepshot. A creepshot captures the natural, raw sexiness of the subject without their vain attempts at putting on a show for the camera. That is the essence of the creepshot, that is what makes a true creepshot worth the effort and that is why this subreddit exists.

Use stealth, cunning and deviousness to capture the beauty of your unsuspecting, chosen target.

Rules. Important!

With the sudden surge in popularity of this subreddit, we have had to implement a new set of rules.

The most important of these is: no suggestive or sexual content featuring minors. Click here for more information. The rest are:

All posts must be Original Content (OC) and of the creeper variety.

Cross[x] posts are acceptable as long as they are OC.

NO UPSKIRT SHOTS This is against the law and forbidden on this subreddit.

No photos taken **on/in/around school settings or of "school girls"** unless you can confirm that they are not minors. Posts that can not be confirmed will be removed.

Don't advertise your own website here.

Do not post pictures of anyone in a situation where they would have a **reasonable expectation of privacy**. This includes anyplace not considered public property, as well as changerooms, washroooms, etc. Sleeping on the couch in your living room? Great, don't post it here. Sunbathing in their backyard? Awesome, don't post it here. This is not a rule, **THIS IS THE LAW**.

A warm and friendly community

There are a few people who have been upset about the content of CreepShots but it is vital for them to remember this: there is nothing illegal about this subreddit whatsoever. We may be immoral, creepy, sinister (some may even accuse us of being 'disturbed') individuals but there is nothing here that breaks any laws. **When you are in public, you do not have a**

reasonable expectation of privacy. We kindly ask women to respect our right to admire your bodies and stop complaining.

We are no different than paparazzi. Except we celebrate beauty without being paid for it.

Rather than condemn our community, why not become a part of it? Feel free to create a Reddit user account and join in our discussions. You will find us to be a warm, friendly, creepy bunch of people.

We are also an active, self-policing site. **Please click here and message the moderators immediately if you find rule-breaking posts.**[17.6]

The photos, including one labeled "Hot Senior Girl in One of My Classes," were posted to the Creepshots subreddit by someone using the ID "WeagleweagleWDE" (Reddit is another service that permits nominally anonymous users). The "Hot Senior Girl" photo was recognized by another student, who posted a comment reading "I know that girl, and I know which teacher you are. I hope you're looking forward to getting fired, you creepy asshole."[17.7]

Internet sleuths quickly helped identify the user as Christopher Bailey, a substitute teacher at East Coweta High School, and they forwarded a bunch of information about

Bailey's online activity to school administrators. Among other things, the information included copies of comments he made about photos posted by school girls, typically in response to the title of their posts. For instance, in response to a post entitled "16 F Asian," WeagleweagleWDE wrote: "You are sexy as fuck.....it's not even fair to the other girls at school how good looking you are." And in response to a post entitled "Totally caught my hot professor staring down my top in class today. Can you blame him? (f)," WeagleweagleWDE replied: "I have to admit as a teacher I do that all the time! Lol....y'all make it so difficult not to look!!!"[17.8]

When confronted by law enforcement, Bailey admitted posting photos of students to the Creepshots subreddit, and he was subsequently fired by the district and investigated by police. An examination of Bailey's cellphone revealed, among other things, that he had been exchanging texts and photos with underage people around the country, including a 16-year-old girl in Ohio that he first met on Reddit.[17.9]

Don't Produce Child Pornography

People who engage in the practice of digital voyeurism may not necessarily intend to create child pornography, but it should come as no great surprise that they frequently do so. Voyeuristic images of children are not automatically considered to be "child pornography," which is generally defined as any sexually explicit image of a child under the age of 18. Such images are presumed to be obscene under federal and state law, and therefore not entitled to First

Amendment protection. A judge or jury can disagree with the prosecutor, or course, but the presumption of illegality is a difficult burden for a defendant to overcome.

What many people do not realize is that a digital image of a clothed minor may still be prosecuted as child pornography if it demonstrates, in the words of the federal child pornography statute, "lascivious exhibition of the genitals or pubic area."[17.10] The decision as to whether to prosecute a voyeuristic image as child pornography will depend on the precise wording of the statute (state or federal) in question and the temperament of the local prosecutor.

Of course, people who engage in digital voyeurism often do intend to create child pornography, either for their personal consumption, or for trading or sale to other child pornographers online. There are numerous cases that illustrate the grim connection among digital imaging devices, the Internet, voyeurism, and child pornography, but few do so more graphically than the arrest and prosecution of Gareth Williams, a popular teacher at the Ysgol Glantaf school in Cardiff, Wales.

In 2010, Canadian investigators raided a company called Azov Films, that specialized in the production and distribution of child exploitation films. Among the records seized were credit card receipts showing that Williams had purchased child exploitation videos from Azov. Following the conviction of the man running Azov, information about his customers was distributed to local law enforcement agencies in over 50 countries around the world.

One of them was the South Wales Police force, which arrested Williams in January 2013 and seized his home computers and various USB devices. A forensics examination revealed over 16,000 images and nearly 700 videos of children either nude or engaged in sexual acts. A number of the videos were particularly disturbing for parents in the community: They appeared to show children using the toilet in a school bathroom at Ysgol Glantaf.

During their raid of Williams's house, police had also discovered "pinhole" camera equipment, and they began a careful examination of the bathrooms in the Ysgol Glantaf school. They eventually found three tiny cameras hidden in a bathroom/changing room: one in the face of a clock, one in an overhead fan, and one in a light switch. Williams admitted using the cameras to secretly film children between the ages of 11–16 over a period of years. He eventually plead guilty to "nine charges of voyeurism, 20 of making indecent photos and two of possessing indecent photos." He was sentenced to five years in prison in May 2014.[17,11]

William's case is extreme but hardly unique. Over the course of 15 years as a computer forensics expert and researcher in the area of cybertraps, I've come across dozens (if not hundreds) of cases of educators producing child pornography, sometimes just for their own use and other times for distribution over the Internet. The production has occurred both in private homes and in school buildings, and is usually uncovered as part of national or international investigation into Web sites where such material is traded and sold. A handful of examples help illustrate the extent of the problem:

- While any involvement by an educator with child pornography is upsetting, the cases that cause the deepest sense of violation and betrayal are those in which teachers who take explicit photos or videos of their students and distribute them to others. One of the most invidious cases in recent memory involved Kimberly Crain, a third-grade teacher in McCloud, Oklahoma. In December 2011, Crain pleaded guilty to 19 counts of sexual exploitation of a child under 12, possessing child pornography, and to lewd molestation. She was arrested after students reported that she took photos and videos of them in their bras and panties during a Christmas tree decorating party at her house. In the subsequent investigation, law enforcement officers discovered a stash of digital photos and videos of her students that Crain had taken in her classroom. Some of the photographs showed girls naked while changing, while others were voyeuristic upskirt photos taken under the desks of students. Crain shared the photos with an acquaintance named Gary Doby, whom the children knew through classroom Skype conversations as "Uncle G." Crain was sentenced to 45 years in prison, and her co-conspirator Doby received a life sentence.[17.12]

- Monmouth Regional High School teacher Cecilia Sneider was arrested in September 2004 and charged with producing child pornography when the police uncovered a photograph of her engaging in a sexual act with a 2-year-old. She later plead guilty to distribution of child pornography and child endangerment.[17.13]

- Richard A. Foster, a teacher at Bradford Elementary School in Bradford, VT, was charged in 2007 with producing child pornography after police received reports from a mother that Foster had sent nude photos of himself to her 12-year-old son. The boy said he sent similar photos to Foster; a subsequent search of Foster's home turned up evidence that he had hidden a video camera under a pile of clothes and recorded a second 12-year-old masturbating in his bedroom. Following a failed suicide attempt, Foster was sentenced to 25 years in prison.[17.14]

- In June 2008, officials at the Beauvoir Elementary School at Washington's National Cathedral discovered sexually explicit photos of a child on a school camera assigned to Eric Justin Toth, a third-grade teacher at the school. In a moment of dubious judgment, the head of the school escorted Toth to the end of the driveway and told him to leave campus immediately. Toth not only left the campus, he fled the country, eventually taking over Osama bin Laden's involuntarily-vacated slot on the FBI's most wanted list. He was apprehended in Nicaragua in April 2013, and is currently awaiting trial on charges of taking nude photos of children in his home and hiding a camera in the bathroom of his school classroom.[17.15]

- In a particularly disturbing and wide-reaching case, a high school dance instructor in the El Paso, TX area named Marco Alferez was arrested on September 30, 2010 on charges of child pornography. When law enforcement officers searched his home and computer, they discovered hundreds of videotapes that Alferez had secretly made of children changing in dressing rooms and engaging in sexual activity with him in his home. He ultimately confessed to making 150 secret videotapes in five area schools, involving just under 400 separate victims. He also admitted to using the peer-to-peer software LimeWire to share the videos with others on the Internet. Alferez was sentenced to 50 years in prison on January 12, 2012.[17.16]

- Steve Orloff, a former director of the special needs program in the Stoneham school district, was charged with posing as a 14-year-old boy online and persuading underage girls to make explicit videos of themselves. He also secretly taped two young female relatives in his home. He hanged himself on

December 14, 2014 while being held at the Essex County House of Corrections.[17,17]

This is an appalling litany, and sadly is just a small fraction of the total number of teacher-related child pornography cases. What should be kept in mind, however, is that these cases, as tragic as they are, represent in turn an even smaller percentage of the dedicated professionals in education who don't abuse their students and aren't attracted to images of underage children. It may not be possible to entirely prevent these types of things from happening, particularly given the ongoing changes in technology, but the goal of every teacher certification program, every licensing board, every school district, and every educator should be to work diligently to lower the number of predators to close to zero as possible.

~~~~~~~~~

Chapter Eighteen
Solicitation, Sexting, and Sexual Assault

As appalling as digital voyeurism and the production of child pornography are, the most serious cybertrap into which an educator can fall is a sexual relationship with a student. Such behavior represents the ultimate betrayal of the confidence and trust which parents place in teachers, that they will safeguard their children's health, safety, and well-being while they get an education. It goes without saying that the victims of childhood abuse often spend decades dealing with the emotional and psychological damage that is inflicted upon them.[18.1]

As I have said throughout this book, the number of teachers who commit offenses (particularly those in the more serious categories I've discussed) are a tiny percentage of the 3 million or so teachers working in the United States, and the millions more working around the world. And without question, headline writers, particularly for anti-union or anti-teacher publications, love to test the concept that "Sex Sells!!" by trumpeting news of teachers assaulting students.

One aspect of recent headline-writing deserves special mention: The disproportionate fondness of tabloids (and even more respectable newspapers) to highlight cases in which a female teacher assaults a male student. There are as yet no good sources of statistical information about the total number of educators who have assaulted students, let alone a specific gender breakdown. Nonetheless, a casual perusal of newspaper headlines would lead you to think that there is an epidemic of female teachers seducing their students. The truth, of course, is more complicated and more difficult to determine. Given the leveling effect of technology and some of the sociological changes that we've seen in the post-Internet era (particularly the easy access to pornography by younger and younger children, let alone adults), I think it is fair to say that the number of female teachers who have assaulted students is rising, and there have been some horrifying examples that make it clear women can be just as predatory as men. At the same time, I believe it is also true that both the actual number and the percentage of female teachers who commit this type of crime still are vastly lower than their male colleagues. Again, it is important to reiterate that regardless of gender, we are talking about a tiny fraction of the total number of educators. Nonetheless, no one should assume that only a certain type of person can be a perpetrator of a sexual assault on a student. Again, evidence disproves any easy assumptions.

Beware the Slippery Slope

In reviewing the various cases in which technology has played a role in the sexual assault of a student, two general patterns emerge. In the first, technology facilitates an initially harmless text or instant messaging conversation that quickly segues into more personal and even sexual topics, with the two sometimes exchanging nude photos as a prelude to a sexual act. The chief characteristic of these "slippery slope" cases is that the educator, after being caught and charged with sexual assault, is stunned to find himself or herself in that position. These types of cases are the most difficult to prevent: Most people can't imagine that they would do anything like that, and their colleagues are usually equally shocked and dismayed. "I can't believe he (or she) would do something like that!" is perhaps the most common reaction.

Unfortunately, the advances in technology over the last twenty years or so (and in particularly in the last decade) have made it far too easy for even the most well-intentioned and well-respected educator to slide down the slippery slope from empathetic teacher to sexual predator. No single change has contributed more to that phenomenon than the fact that every child who gets a cellphone now has their own personal phone number that permits anyone with that number to contact them directly, regardless of the time of day or night. On top of that, the vast majority of teens have accounts on multiple social media Web sites and smartphone apps, opening myriad channels of unsupervised communication between the teen and the rest of the world. And unfortunately, all too many children have unfettered use of their electronic devices all night long, so any communication by an educator to a student after 9 or 10pm almost certainly goes straight to the student's bedroom. Taken together, these developments have badly weakened the traditional boundaries between teachers and students.

The steepness of the slippery slope is amply illustrated by the case of Alicia Gray, a 28-year-old former math teacher at

Mary G. Montgomery High School in Mobile, AL. On New Year's Day in 2013, she began exchanging messages with a 14-year-old boy in the school via Facebook, text messages, and online services. The messages quickly grew more serious and flirtatious, and not long afterwards, the two engaged in oral sex "near or at the victim's home."[18.2] A school counselor notified the Mobile County Sheriffs Office in mid-February about possible abuse of a child and Gray was immediately placed on paid administrative leave pending an investigation. Police officers interviewed the boy and discovered nude photos on his cellphone that Gray had taken of herself and sent to the boy.[18.3]

Gray turned herself into police on February 25, 2013, and was charged with "two counts of second-degree sodomy, one count of second-degree sexual abuse and one count of being a school employee who had sexual contact with a student under the age of 19."[18.4] Nine months later, she accepted a plea deal in which she admitted to a single charge of "engaging in a sexual act or deviant sexual intercourse with a student under 19 years old." She was sentenced to a five-year split sentence, consisting of six months in prison and five years' probation. She also agreed to surrender her teaching certificate.[18.5] In a somewhat unusual step, Gray recorded and released a video apology just prior to reporting to jail.

Another torrid affair came to light in Chelmsford, England, when teaching assistant Charlotte Parker was arrested for having a 2-year affair with a student starting when he was 14. The boy first sent a harmless Christmas card to his teacher, but then the two began to exchange increasingly explicit messages using the WhatsApp smartphone app. Over one 3-week stretch in 2013, the pair exchanged more than 3,000 messages. Forensic analysis of devices seized from Parker's home showed more exchanges, as well as nude photos that had been taken of the boy.[18.6] Remarkably, Parker avoided jail time despite pleading guilty to three counts of sexual activity with a child. In part because the judge described the 14-year-old boy as a "willing participant," she received a 3-year suspended sentence. However she was also banned from teaching for life and was ordered to register as a sex offender for a decade.[18.7]

Predatory Teachers

Sometimes, it is difficult to determine whether a teacher has slid down the slippery slope, or is someone who fits the second general pattern, the active predator who uses technology to groom one or more students in preparation for a sexual assault. The sad and unavoidable truth is that there is some small percentage of educators who actively seek to abuse the children they teach, a goal which technology makes much easier than it was in the past. Communication tools like text messages and Facebook can create a rapid sense of intimacy (particularly when conversations take place late at night), which a predator can use to seduce a victim.

A classic example occurred during the 2013-2014 school year at Hedgesville High School in Hedgesville, WV. A freshman girl and her boyfriend told the local police in June

2014 that they were receiving threatening messages on Facebook from Erin Steve Thomas, a teacher at the school. The girl testified that when she started high school in the fall of 2013, she was "kind of a loner." Thomas befriended the girl, and they began having conversations on Facebook, with Thomas using a fake account that he had created. Over a period of months, they began exchanging gifts, kissed, and eventually progressed to sexual contact. The girl tried to break off the relationship after Thomas's wife found out, but he became jealous of her new boyfriend and started threatening them.[18.8] Thomas was indicted three months later on 7 counts of sexual assault and fired from his teaching position.[18.9]

Another alleged predator, Joaquim Andrade, a teacher of English as a Second Language at Brockton High School, MA, is facing charges that he set up a fake Facebook account to converse with a 14-year-old female student about school soccer. He allegedly offered to drive her to a school soccer match one day, but after picking her up, took her to a different location and sexually assaulted her before dropping her off at the game. He is currently facing charges of "rape with force, aggravated rape, two counts of indecent assault and battery of a child over 14 and enticement of a child under 16."[18.10]

And then there's the case of Zachary Josh Reeder, a former history teacher at Servite High School in Anaheim, CA. On January 29, 2014, Reeder was sentenced to 10 years in prison and lifetime sex offender registration for "four felony counts of distributing pornography to a minor, two felony counts of lewd acts upon a child under 14, two felony counts of contacting a child with the intent to commit a lewd act, one felony count each of using a minor for sex acts, lewd act upon a child, possession and control of child pornography, and distribution of child pornography."

The charges were based on the results of an investigation that showed that Reeder had created a fake Facebook page to pose as a 14-year-old girl. He used that profile to befriend more than 100 boys aged 13–17 in four area high schools and persuade them to send him sexually explicit photos and videos. As one of the victim impact statements poignantly said, "My young son was deceived and no match for the manipulation and intent of the accused. He used his adult influences to attract young, vulnerable boys that respected him for his own sexual enjoyment using social media."[18.11]

What is particularly frustrating for school districts, administrators, and parents is that the vast array of communication tools and their widespread use by teens has made it so much easier for predators to lure and groom vulnerable students without being detected. There is no easy solution; if someone is committed to assaulting students, they will go to extraordinary lengths to hide their intent and achieve their goal. The best that we can do is to remind educators of the life-destroying consequences of committing these acts, educate students about potential risks and what they can do to avoid them, and as adults, respond promptly and honestly (no "passing the trash") to any reports of student abuse.

~~~~~~~~~~

Section IV
Teacher Precautions and Solutions

~~~~~~~~

Frederick S. Lane

Chapter Nineteen
"THINK!"

More than 100 years ago, a sales manager for the National Cash Register Company named Thomas J. Watson, Sr. coined a new motto to inspire his sales staff: "THINK". That one word, scribbled on an easel during a sales meeting, eventually became the motto of one of the world's leading computer companies: IBM, which Watson was chosen to run in 1914.[191] While head of IBM, Watson had posters and signs printed up and plastered around IBM facilities, reminding his employees that they "get paid for working with [their] heads." The company eventually trademarked the slogan and incorporated it into its current line of laptops, the ThinkPad.

Watson's maxim may seem elementary, but it's good advice for everyone, and particularly for those who work in the public sphere. If you are going to be an educator, or if you already are one, then you need to THINK carefully about three different categories of online information: your cyberpast, your cyberpresent (and cyberpresence), and your cyberfuture.

Your Cyberpast

As we saw in the earlier sections about cybertraps outside of the workplace, it is all too easy for students, parents, and administrators to research what you did before becoming an educator. On a fairly regular basis, you should do the same thing; search for yourself on Google, Bing, Facebook,

Twitter, and other Web search sites to see what comes up. Not only might there be things that you've forgotten about, but new information is constantly being added and indexed every day. It's good to know what's out there.

Can you get something removed from the Internet? Possibly, but probably not. If it's information you own (for instance, someone hacks your online photos or uploads stolen images from your phone), then you do have a legal right to the removal of the information. But that's different from the practical removal of information; if the information that you want removed is in any way salacious, the odds are very good that it has been copied hundreds, if not thousands of times, and has spread throughout the Internet. And of course, if you signed a contract allowing electronic distribution (for instance, if you once modeled for *Playboy*), or the information is some type of public record or news report, then the answer almost certainly will be no.

You will have more success removing information you control (embarrassing social media posts, for instance) or information posted by someone you know (a friend who tagged you in a photo at the beach party you don't remember very well). In the former case, it's your responsibility to know what's in your social media feeds and make a decision as to whether it reflects who you are now. (This type of review is particularly important now that Facebook has made it possible to search for old posts.) In the latter case, a simple polite request to a "friend" will usually suffice, since you might have to return the favor for them some day.

There are a number of companies online that offer, for a fee, to assist you in cleaning up your embarrassing Internet history. Many of them are outright scams, since they overpromise and underdeliver; they won't be any more successful removing content owned by someone else than you would be. You may have lived a spotless life online and off, but if not, the best approach is to acknowledge the choices you've made and let your employer know before some kid in the third row holds up his hand and asks, "Hey, is this you??!!"

Your Cyberpresent and (Cyberpresence)

If you're reading this in your pre-licensure program, then this is a good time to reflect on the technologies that you currently use in your everyday life. The odds are good that you'll need to make some adjustments. For instance, are you an inveterate social media user? Do you blog frequently? Is much of your life lived on Instagram? Take the time to do a brief but accurate inventory of the devices, applications, Web sites, and computer programs that you use daily or weekly.

Once you've accomplished that, take a close look at **how** you use those devices. What kind of information do you share, with whom do you share it, and when? If you discover that you have a history of posting salacious Instagram photos after midnight, or engaging in long-running drunken Twitter insult battles with your old frat buddies, then it's time to realize that your relationship with social media (and your friends) will have to change now that you have decided to become (or perhaps already are) a licensed teacher.

For both pre-licensure and established teachers, it's a good idea to periodically do a search of yourself online. Type your name into two or three different search engines to see what comes up, and also try adding keywords such as your hometown or the schools you have attended (particularly if you have a common name). This is especially important if you are in the pre-licensure stage, since there is a very strong likelihood that the human resources departments of the districts to which you apply will be doing exactly the same thing. People who search for you can form a pretty powerful impression of you from the first page or two of search results associated with your name, much in the same way that people make an initial assessment of how you're dressed when you walk into a job interview. If there is something unpleasant or unprofessional that turns up when you do a self-search, hopefully you'll have the time to either try to remove it, which can be difficult, or prepare an explanation. If there's one upside to all of this, it's that an increasing number of interviewers (and even administrators) have their own social media horror stories.

Even after you've successfully landed a teaching job, you should still periodically do a self-search. As you go through your career, it is important to keep tabs on the digital profile that you are presenting to the world. Don't forget that new information is being added to the Internet all the time. Search engines are constantly indexing new information, so your profile will not remain static.

Your Cyberfuture

Given the inherent impossibility, it's really pretty amazing how much time people spend trying to predict the future. Most of the time, we can't successfully predict next year's iPhone features, let alone anything more substantive. But trends are somewhat easier to spot, and there are two on which all educators should keep a close eye.

First, the infiltration of the Internet into our daily lives will steadily accelerate, by which I mean the collection of data, the ubiquity of social media, the indexing of information, *etc*. Already, data about our lives is being collected by a staggering array of governmental agencies, corporations both online and off, and the myriad devices that we carry with us nearly every minute of the day. For good reason, many question whether our ability to control the information we generate, the core concept of personal privacy, has been irrevocably lost. The jury may still be out on that question, but the future is not promising. For educators (and other public figures like politicians, celebrities, and so on), the already tiny zone of privacy will continue to shrink even further.

Second, the technology that leads to many of the cybertraps discussed earlier will only get smaller, faster, and cheaper. Educators will need to be continually wary of the temptations that these new technologies present. As we've seen, shrinking camera sizes have already induced some educators into a level of voyeurism that they might never otherwise have attempted with larger or louder cameras.

These are not developments that can be reversed by a single individual, much like global warming or airline consolidation. But you can make individual decisions that improve or worsen your position relative to those trends.

~~~~~~~~~

Chapter Twenty
Choose Your Friends Carefully

Repeat after me: Facebook is not your friend. Mark Zuckerberg and Melissa Meyers are not your friends. In fact, no social media service or social media executive is your friend. Their job is not to be your friend, but instead, to figure out how to make their companies profitable so that they won't be savaged by financial analysts on CNBC (who are not their friends either).

Social media sites are busily trying to figure out exactly how to be profitable, but there is one thing that is an essential part of every conceivably viable business plan: your information—all of the information that you post online, how often and with whom you share, the identity of your friends, the information they share with you, the information of yours that they share with THEIR friends, and so on, and so on, *ad infinitum*. What this means in practical terms is that social media companies want you to have a large friend/follower list, and want you to share as much information as possible with all of them. But if you're an educator, that's not in your best interest.

Here's just one piece of the problem: Facebook, chief among the social media services, has persuaded over one-seventh of the world's entire population that its social media service is the equivalent of an electronic diary for its users, a place where we can record our thoughts, our dreams, our political opinions, *etc.* But it's not really a diary; instead, it's our own personal newspaper that can be read by our friends, their friends, or the entire world, depending on privacy settings (which of course can be easily breached, thanks to screen capture and other easy-to-use techniques). Facebook's goal, one that it has largely succeeded in achieving, is to make the act of updating our "status" so automatic (you can even do it with your cellphone!), that we don't engage whatever internal filters we might have to determine whether we SHOULD update our status.

Given the corporate and social pressures associated with social media, accidents will happen, and educators will post things that they should not. If you don't want to be one of the educators who winds up on the front page of the *Huffington Post* or the *Daily Mail*, then you need to give some thought to structural changes in your social media habits that will reduce the likelihood of permanent Internet infamy.

Pay Close Attention to Privacy Settings

Obviously, the first step is understand and implement the privacy setting that are available to you. Facebook has taken a lot of (justifiable) abuse over the years for its slow and erratic implementation of privacy controls, but over time, it has actually developed a fairly effective privacy suite for its users. The starting place is Facebook's own page on data use policy, but its very thoroughness is a little daunting. A better approach might be to Google the terms "recommended Facebook privacy settings" and read summaries from trusted sources like Lifehacker (one of my favorite sites) or

AllFacebook, "the Unofficial Facebook Blog". With just an hour or two of reading, you can significantly improve your privacy on Facebook or any other social media service you use. Just do it. This isn't foolproof, but it does help.

Keep Your Friend Lists as Small as Possible

As should be evident from the experiences of Ashley Payne, Christina Rubino, and others, every additional virtual "friend" that you have on social media increases the odds that if you make a mistake online, it will become a much bigger deal than you want it to be. As awkward as it may seem, try to envision posting updates to your social media friends list in physical terms: would you be comfortable standing up in front of an equivalent number of people and ranting about your students? At most, you might be willing to vent to a large dinner party or even a small cocktail gathering, but even then, you'd see from their reactions that not everyone approves of what you're saying. You might actually worry that someone would repeat it to a parent, or maybe your building principal.

If you work as a teacher or administrator, you have two choices: either pay VERY close attention to what you post online, all the time, or make sure that your friend or follower list is composed of actual friends who are more likely to know when you are joking or just blowing off steam. Since we all make mistakes, or have such bad days that our self-control is overwhelmed, the first approach may not be practical. The second approach may feel more limiting, but it ultimately offers you more protection and ironically, more freedom. There's a simple litmus test for each person: is he or she someone you would be comfortable sharing your true feelings about the little urchins you teach over a cup of coffee or a glass of wine? If not, then just don't include them on your friend list.

Use Social Media to Separate Your Acquaintances and Colleagues from Your Friends

Another approach that can help protect you from the unintended consequences of social media is to use different social media services or technologies for communicating with different groups of people. Your personal communication protocol could look something like this:

- Phone: personal and confidential discussions with family members and adult friends;
- Text Messages: personal and confidential messages to family members and adult friends;
- Email: personal and professional correspondence, and communication with students only if through a school email system;
- Facebook: personal communication with family and close friends [no students];
- LinkedIn: professional communication with acquaintances and colleagues [no students];

You should see a common theme here: do not communicate electronically with students unless there is transparency: a digital archive of emails, at least one other adult in a text message group, a school-run Facebook page, *etc.* The reality is that all forms of electronic communication—and particularly social media—are inherently slippery slopes, particularly when students are involved. With the pace of life (and communication) constantly accelerating, the best way to protect yourself is to THINK ahead of time about what you want to say, to whom you want to say it, and the possible consequences of clicking "Send." Whatever you do, always operate under the assumption that there is no privacy in any cybersphere, and that every keystroke and mouse click you make can be held against you.

~~~~~~~~

Frederick S. Lane

Chapter Twenty-One
Students Are Not Your Friends

Most of the educators that I've met over the years (including various family members) chose to enter the profession because they have a genuine, even passionate desire to teach kids and help them achieve their potential. A significant part of being a good teacher, particularly during high school, is the ability to communicate with sometimes surly and hormonally volatile children, and to empathize with them about the challenges they face as they transition to adulthood.

As my friend and colleague Troy Hutchings often points out in his lectures, all too often it is the teachers who are the most empathetic and the most successful in communicating with students who are the ones most at risk for the boundary violations I discussed earlier. Their overwhelming desire to mentor and to help can all too easily create an emotional bond that in turn can lead to inappropriate communication and then to an inappropriate relationship.

There's no way to completely prevent that from ever happening. As Woody Allen said in an infamous interview in *Time* about his relationship with ex-lover Mia Farrow's adopted daughter Soon-Yi Previn, "The heart wants what it wants. There's no logic to those things. You meet someone and you fall in love and that's that."[21.1] But if you find yourself so attracted to a student that you are thinking of entering into a romantic or sexual relationship, then it's fair to ask whether it is your heart or some other body part that wants what it wants. And even if it is your heart that's speaking, is it speaking from a place of wholeness and strength, or is it looking to fill some lack created by another part of your life? Since nearly every teacher who is caught sleeping with a student is ordered to get mental health treatment, maybe the better approach is to seek help before violating the profound obligation you have taken on as an educator.

Be Mindful

Perhaps, as you have reviewed the examples of teachers who have been fired or who have lost their license as a result of electronic misconduct, it was tempting to think that it could never happen to you. I'm sure that many of the teachers I've discussed in this book had precisely the same thought. But many adults go through phases of their lives during which they are more vulnerable and needy, and more at risk of doing something they will later regret. The first step in avoiding the various cybertraps that I've described is to simply be aware of what they are, and how easily they can happen.

It's also important to pay attention to your own mental and emotional state. Assuming for the moment that you're not an innate predator, the challenge is to know when you might be potentially be vulnerable to an inappropriate relationship with a student. A little earlier, I talked about the importance of periodically doing a search to see what information has been posted online. You should also periodically evaluate how you are mentally and emotionally coping with the various stresses in your life, both in and out of the classroom. Seek help proactively, especially if you feel your professional and personal boundaries beginning to erode.

Be Transparent

One of the critical warning signs that your interaction with a student is heading into dangerous territory is a growing desire to keep your communication with the student secret. Unfortunately, the technological tools available today make it much easier and more tempting to engage in seemingly private conversations with students. The phone is a perfect example. Twenty years ago, the only way to talk with a student by phone was to call the landline at his or her home (and of course, nobody thought of it as a "landline" back then). The odds were fairly good, particularly at night, that the phone would be answered by a parent, who understandably would be curious as to why a teacher was calling the house.

Today, of course, the vast majority of high school and middle school students have their own cellphones, which makes it possible for them to have one-to-one communication with anyone who has their phone number. Unwittingly, parents have largely cut themselves out of the communication loop, and have made it possible for their children to receive calls and messages at all times of the day and night, and in all locations, including their bedrooms.

If you are going to communicate with a student electronically, then I strongly believe that it should be through a mediated service, one that others have access to at the same time. Some examples might include:

- The school email system, where a copy of all emails is stored on the school servers;

- Private email, but only if the student's parents are copied on all correspondence;

- Texting, but again, only if parents are included in a group message; and

- A Facebook or other social media group set up for an entire class, with access by school administrators and/or parents.

Obvious things to avoid include: one-to-one text messages; private chats on Facebook or other messenger services; direct messages on Twitter; surreptitious email accounts; and so on. If you find yourself doing any of these things (or some variant that pops up in the future), then you should be questioning your motivations and your commitment to remaining an educator. If these are impulses that you don't feel you can restrain, a new career may be your smartest choice.

Having had numerous discussions about this with educators around the country, I know that some people passionately believe that it is important to communicate with kids in the manner in which kids themselves are most comfortable communicating; it's hard enough, they argue, to find out what kids are thinking without trying to force them to use communication tools that they feel are hopelessly outdated (like email).

I understand that argument; I know, for instance, that my odds of getting a response from one of my sons rises dramatically if I just send them a text message. But there are two reasons, I think, for school boards and administrators to draw a line in the sand on this issue.

First, I think that the risks for educators far outweigh the rewards. In today's climate, it is far too easy for parents or colleagues to draw the wrong conclusion if they discover that you are engaging in private or secretive communication with a particular student. You may have the best of intentions, but it still looks bad.

Second, transparent communication is much more likely to be professional communication. If you know that other people can read what you've written and associate it with your name, you are much less likely to start segueing into more personal areas of a student's life. Again, I know that many teachers feel that it is important to give students an emotional outlet when they're having a difficult time, but the reality is that educators are trained to teach, not do social work, counseling, or therapy. There's a little of that in virtually every teacher's day, of course, but everyone is better off, and safer, if strict boundaries are observed, and trained experts are called in to take over when students need help with personal situations.

Frederick S. Lane

~~~~~~~~

Chapter Twenty-Two
Be a Role Model for Good Online Behavior

The expectation that teachers will serve as positive role models for their students is long-established and not likely to significantly diminish in the near future. Frankly, that's not the worst thing in the world. Students can always benefit from additional positive role models, particularly as society attempts to navigate the rocky transition to an increasingly digital world. Educators have the twin advantages of authority and a captive audience. Given that children spend as much time or more in school than they do at home, it's not unreasonable to expect that school districts and educators should play an active role in raising good cybercitizens.

If you plan to become or remain an educator, you should be realistic about the expectation on the part of your school district, parents, and the community that you will in fact be a positive role model for your students, particularly with respect to your online behavior. Here are a few suggestions on how to do that.

Be a Professional

The starting place for being a positive digital role model is in your overall demeanor and your real-life interpersonal communications. Educators have spent decades in an effort to establish that teaching is a **profession**, and so there is a reasonable expectation that you will conduct yourself in a professional manner when dealing with students, whether online or off. They will notice when you don't, and react accordingly.

Communicate Like a Professional

I don't think that there's much question that most educators understand the basics of dealing professionally with parents and students in real life, but society has not had much time to develop similar norms for online communications. One of the many risks of engaging students through unmediated, non-transparent, one-to-one communication channels is the inherent damage to your aura of professionalism, wholly apart from what you actually say or do.

In the most charitable of interpretations, of course, it's an inherently empathetic act: You are saying to the student, "Hey, I'll use **Facebook** or **WhatsApp** or **Instagram** to communicate with you on *your* level because that's where you're most comfortable, and I know that you really need a friendly adult in your life." It's a natural impulse, particularly for the types of educators who crave popularity with students.

That same impulse, however, implicitly undercuts key elements of professionalism: not only authority and respect, but the more intangible distance and objectivity that are a natural (and deserved) by-product of training in a particular field. If you and a student are goofing around together on social media at 11:30 at night (or even 4:30 in the afternoon), it's much more difficult to maintain an appropriate teacher-student relationship in the classroom.

Communicate About Professional Topics

The Internet has created numerous profound benefits for educators: every day, teachers can tap into a rapidly-expanding universe of information and knowledge to help enrich their lesson plans. At the same time, however, teachers face the same risks that we all face: distraction, wasted time, and sheer inappropriateness.

That's one of the benefits of only using mediated channels to communicate with students and their parents: If you don't behave as a professional when you're posting on a shared Facebook page or in a multi-person email, you know that someone will object and probably fairly quickly. The awareness that a wide audience, including supervisors, is reading your posts significantly reduces the likelihood that you will bad-mouth other teachers, gossip about students, share dirty or inappropriate jokes, or circulate videos of cats riding a Roomba, photos of bikini-clad women, or the latest shot of David Beckham in his briefs. As an educator, you probably shouldn't be sending such things even to your private and tightly-limited social media friends, but such content is of course not remotely appropriate for publication to students and/or their parents.

~~~~~~~~~~

Chapter Twenty-Three
Be an Advocate for Good District Policies, Procedures, and Practices

Beyond being a good digital role model for students, the best thing that any educator can do is to advocate for good district policies, procedures, and practices that can, among other things, help to affirm educator professionalism, protect your due process rights, and promote confidence in the public schools and the people who teach in them. It is not easy to find the time to do all this, obviously, but it is essential work.

Policy advocacy is particularly important with respect to how educators should use technology in and out of the classroom. The standards and best practices for such use are constantly evolving, as new hardware and software is introduced on a regular basis. Educators should be at the forefront of discussions regarding how various technologies can enhance the learning process and aid their students, without crossing important boundaries and damaging educator professionalism.

It's often difficult for newly-minted or inexperienced teachers to find ways to influence district policies. Technology, however, is a field in which even the most fresh-faced educators can have a significant impact on policy debates. Younger educators bring a number of important advantages to the table: They tend to have a much greater familiarity with recent and emerging technologies; they are generally more familiar with how those technologies are being put to use by their students, who are often not that much younger than they are; and increasingly, they can talk about and apply their personal experience of being educated in a post-World Wide Web world.

In order to be an effective advocate for good cyberpolicies, some homework is necessary. Here are the two important topics that are worth researching:

What Rules Are in Place Now?

The first and most important step is to determine if there are any policies or procedures relating to the use of technology, and if so, to familiarize yourself with them. Even now, two decades into the World Wide Web, it is still possible that you work in a district that has not adopted formal policies regarding the use of technology. The more likely scenario, however, is that you will discover that your district does have policies and procedures in place. Those policies and procedures may have been rendered obsolete by changes in technology, ranging from upgrades to hardware to the introduction of new apps and Web sites.

If your research reveals that your district's policies and procedures are non-existent, inadequate or simply outdated, then do yourself and your colleagues a favor, and start the ball rolling to discuss and update the rules of the cyber road.

What Changes Are Needed?

The great majority of public school districts, charter schools, and private schools have at least some basic policies relating to acceptable use, integration of technology in the classroom, incident response, *etc.* Perhaps the gold standard in this regard, predictably enough, is the Palo Alto Unified School District in the heart of California's Silicon Valley. On its Web site, it has a page dedicated to "Technology Policies and Guidelines," with the following entries:

- Employee Use of Technology;
- District Technology Plan;
- Acceptable Use Agreements for:
    - Staff Full Access
    - Staff Limited Access, and
    - Non-Employees
- General Policies, including:
    - Copyright in Web Development;
    - Mission and Principles for Web Development;
    - Responsibilities of Web Development; and
    - Terms of Use
- Guest Wireless;
- Student Technology Handbook (in English and Spanish); and
- Student Acceptable Use of PAUSD Student Wireless Network.

Not every district, obviously, needs to take such a comprehensive approach to technology management and supervision (at least right now). But every district does need to have some conversation about these issues and adopt some basic guidelines to govern the use and prevent the misuse of digital technology.

How Is Change Accomplished in My District?

If the answer to this question is something like "No change ever occurs in my district," then it's fair to consider whether you need to change districts instead of trying to change the district you're in. But if moving to another district is simply not an option, then it is worth spending some time and effort to make your district more tech-friendly and tech-savvy.

Being an advocated for better district technology policies is hardly a guarantee against stumbling into one or more of the cybertraps I've discussed in this book. Very few people get through an entire professional career without a stumble of one sort or another. Nonetheless, understanding your district's policies well enough to advocate for change and improvement will not only make things better for your colleagues and your students, but will serve as a frequent reminder of the standards of cyberethical behavior that you yourself should be following.

Conclusion

Sometimes, it is all too easy to sympathize with parents who leave my lectures shaking their heads and muttering that they're going to lock up every piece of digital technology in their house. But that's not a realistic option for parents, let alone for entire school districts that are charged, among other things, with helping to prepare students to work in a digital world.

At the same time, we can't ignore the fact that technology has assisted people in causing real harm to others, and that it is our responsibility to do everything we can to prevent that harm from occurring (or at least minimize its incidence). There is no single solution that will achieve that goal, but there are a variety of steps that we can and should take. These include (but are not limited to):

- Develop and implement a comprehensive K-12 digital citizenship curriculum to educate students about the unique risks they face from the use and misuse of electronic devices;

- Develop and implement a national code of ethics for the teaching profession and including a strong digital component, again to underscore the unique risks posed by technology;

- Require annual professional development programs to remind educators of the cybertraps posed by technology, to educate them about new types of hardware and software, and to alert them to new ways in which students are using technology;

- Help educate parents about the role that students play in creating cybertraps for educators and remind them that they may be liable for their child's malicious acts;

- Develop a national clearinghouse to help catalog cases in which educators misuse technology, to better understand the extent to which these problems are occurring, the types of technology being used, and the impact on victims; and

- Insist that districts be held accountable when they cover up instances of educator misconduct and "pass the trash" to other unsuspecting districts.

Many of these initiatives, fortunately, are already underway in programs large and small around the world. It is a privilege to be part of this work.

Acknowledgments

Following the 2011 publication of my previous book, <u>*Cybertraps for the Young*</u>, I had the good fortune to meet one of the leading scholars on teacher ethics in the United States, Dr. Troy Ray Hutchings, who serves as Research Chair for the College of Education and School of Advanced Studies at the University of Phoenix. He invited me to present a lecture based on my book at the annual meeting of the Professional Practices Institute (PPI) in Little Rock, Arkansas. PPI is an off-shoot of the National Association of State Directors of Teacher Education and Certification; both organizations are composed of dozens, if not hundreds, of dedicated education professionals from around the United States and Canada. Although I had planned to begin work on *Cybertraps for Educators* even before meeting Troy, I am deeply grateful that he introduced me to these terrific communities. They (along with Troy himself) have proven to be invaluable resources as I have worked on this book.

Through Troy, I also had the pleasure of meeting Dr. Glenn Scott Lipson, a forensic psychologist and program director of the California School of Forensic Science at Alliant International University. Glenn has played a leading role in promoting child safety in schools over the last several decades, and his encouragement during the drafting of this book has been tremendously helpful. I have had the opportunity to collaborate with Glenn over the last couple of years on several lectures and presentations, and it is an honor to do so. He is passionate about improving the tools that school districts and law enforcement use to prevent harm to students, and I hope that this book will further those goals.

Over the past three years, I've attended several PPI and NASDTEC events, and have had too many useful and thought-provoking conversations to enumerate individually. But I would like to extend my particular thanks to Phillip Rogers, Carolyn Angelo, Marian Lambeth, Catherine Slagle, Michael L. Smith, Lynn Hammonds, Nadine Carpenter, Joe Jamieson, and Terri Miller for their encouragement, their interest, and their enthusiasm for this project.

Through PPI member Pat Trueman, I had the pleasure of participating in 2012 annual conference of the Alaska Society for Technology in Education (ASTE). Apart from the sheer delight of visiting Alaska, it was a great introduction to a particularly dedicated group of educators grappling with the issues raised by the use of technology in the classroom and the challenges of long-distance learning. Among the organizers was Keith Zamudio, the technology coordinator for the Cordova School District, who has been a big help with various aspects of this project. Keith and his wife Kathy also were kind enough to host me on a return lecture trip to area school districts, and helped introduce me to the highly enjoyable (if somewhat frustrating) sport of salmon fishing in between presentations. I would also like to express my gratitude to other members of the Alaskan educational community, including Eugenie Sadler, Mary Wegener, Jim Seitz, Jill Rusyniak, Lee Graham, Rod Schug, and Robin Gray.

Much of my interest in education and appreciation for the challenging job teachers face comes from my decade of service on the Burlington School Board. During my time on the Board, I had a chance to discuss various cyberissues with a large number of interesting and dedicated educational professionals, as well as my fellow board members. I am particularly appreciative of my many conversations with Superintendents Lyman Amsden and Jeanne Collins, Assistant Superintendent Terry Bailey, IT Director Paul Irish, HR Director Sara Jane Mahan, HS Principal Amy Mellencamp, Board Counsel Joe McNeil, former Chairs Paul Hale and Thom Fleury, and board members Keith Pillsbury, Amy Werbel, Bernie O'Rourke, and Kathy Chasan.

Warm thanks are due to Harvey and Glenda Werbel, at whose house this book was started and finished. I would also like to extend my ongoing thanks and gratitude to my parents, Warren and Anne Lane, for their steadfast enthusiasm for my work, and to a terrific group of siblings: Jonathan Lane, Elizabeth Murdock, and Kate Van Sleet.

I am particularly blessed to have the love and companionship of my wife, Dr. Amy Werbel, and our four sons, Ben, Graham, Peter, and Emmett. It a rare thing for a writer to not only have someone to provide such strong encouragement and support throughout the often-challenging book-writing process, but also someone who can provide top-flight editing assistance when the writing finally grinds to a conclusion. This book is far better for her careful reading and thoughtful suggestions, and I am eternally grateful.

~~~~~~~~~~

Endnotes

The material referenced in these endnotes is drawn from my research files, which have been compiled over the past fifteen years. In many cases, I have copies of articles which may have been moved from the original electronic location, or which may be from sources that no longer exist. Every effort has been made to provide thorough and accurate citations, but inevitably, it may not be possible to access some of these articles directly. If anyone is attempting to locate a cited article that cannot be found online, please contact the author.

1.1. Darren Evans, "Swell of Support for Surfing Teacher," *TES Connect*, January 9, 2009 [http://www.tes.co.uk/article.aspx?storycode=6006921].

1.2. Lucy Kellaway, "I can't stop my cyber loafing," Financial Times, February 24, 2013 [http://www.ft.com/intl/cms/s/0/37a5b704-7b5d-11e2-8eed-00144feabdc0.html] (registration required).

1.3. "Web Surfing 'as Addictive as Coffee,'" CNN.com International, May 19, 2005 [http://edition.cnn.com/2005/BUSINESS/05/19/web.work/index.html]. In a sign of how different the Web was back then, "social media" didn't even make the top five reasons for personal Web use; the leading categories were "news sites (81 percent), personal email (61 percent), online banking (58 percent), travel (56 percent) and shopping (52 percent)."

1.4. *Id.*

1.5. Anthony Wing Kosner, "The Internet of Things: Apple's iBeacon Is Already in Almost 200 Million iPhones and iPads," Forbes, December 15, 2013 [http://www.forbes.com/sites/anthonykosner/2013/12/15/the-internet-of-ithings-apples-ibeacon-is-already-in-almost-200-million-iphones-and-ipads/].

1.6. *See, e.g.*, Jill Hare, "Top Ten Ways to Get Fired," Teaching.Monster.com, n.d. [Last accessed December 3, 2014, at http://teaching.monster.com/careers/articles/7342-top-10-ways-to-get-fired].

1.7. Richard Savill, "Teacher Surfed Facebook and eBay During Class Time, Disciplinary Hearing Told," *The Telegraph*, November 25, 2008 [http://www.telegraph.co.uk/education/educationnews/3520409/Teacher-surfed-Facebook-and-eBay-during-class-time-disciplinary-hearing-told.html].

1.8. *Id.*

1.9. "Web misuse teacher can work again," BBC News, November 26, 2008 [http://news.bbc.co.uk/2/hi/7750218.stm].

1.10. Darren Evans, "Swell of Support for Surfing Teacher," *TES Connect*, January 9, 2009 [http://www.tes.co.uk/article.aspx?storycode=6006921].

1.11. *Id.*

1.12. Leslie Williams Hale, "Lee school employee accused of surfing Web while two students in his care engage in sex acts," *Naples Daily News*, May 1, 2009 [Last accessed

on 3 December 2014 at
http://www.naplesnews.com/news/education/lee-school-employee-accused-surfing-web-while-two-].

1.13. Special School Board Meeting - MINUTES, The School Board of Lee County, November 17, 2009 [Last accessed on 3 December 2014 at
http://www.leeschools.net/board/board_minutes/09-10/111709_special.pdf].

2.1. National Education Association, "Model Language Regarding Protecting Members Rights to a Workplace Free of Bullying or Harassment," April 2013 [
http://www.nea.org/home/55743.htm].

2.2. Liz Hochstedler, "Update: Teacher Created Hostile Work Environment," *The Chippewa Herald*, August 28, 2010 [http://chippewa.com/news/local/update-teacher-created-hostile-work-environment/article_3fe8fcce-b250-11df-a07f-001cc4c002e0.html].

2.3. *Id.*

2.4. Liz Hochstedler, "McElhenny Filed Injunction to Keep Records Secret," *The Chippewa Herald*, August 28, 2010 [http://chippewa.com/news/local/mcelhenny-filed-injunction-to-keep-records-secret/article_341852e6-b250-11df-b892-001cc4c002e0.html].

2.5. "McElhenny Withdraws from School Board Race," *The Chippewa Herald*, March 11, 2011 [
http://chippewa.com/news/local/mcelhenny-withdraws-from-

school-board-race/article_fda4f02c-4b9a-11e0-97b1-001cc4c03286.html].

2.6. *See* Lane, Frederick S. *The Naked Employee: How Technology Is Compromising Workplace Privacy.* New York: Amacom Books, 2003.

2.7. "67% of Bosses Say They Have Caught Employees Looking at Porn whilst at Work," *Yahoo! Finance,* September 10, 2013 [http://finance.yahoo.com/news/67-bosses-caught-employees-looking-070000946.html].

2.8. Mark Hachman, "Study: Employees Sneak Peeks at Videos at Work, Even Porn," PCMag.com, July 12, 2011 [http://www.pcmag.com/article2/0,2817,2388366,00.asp].

2.9. Ki Mae Huessner and Matthew Jaffe, "How Big Is the SEC's Porn Problem?" *ABC News,* March 25, 2010 [http://abcnews.go.com/Technology/big-secs-porn-problem/story?id=10193518].

2.10. Lynne Curry, "Hostile Environment: Porn in the Workplace—More Often than We Know," *HR Gazette*, April 3, 2013 [http://www.hrgazette.com/hostile-environment-porn-in-the-workplace-more-often-than-we-know/].

2.11. Anne Sewell, "Teacher in Germany Caught Watching Porn in Class by Students," *Digital Journal*, November 19, 2013 [http://digitaljournal.com/article/362435].

2.12. Andrew Hough, "Reynella East College 'Violent Porn Teacher' under Formal Investigation from Teachers Registration Board," *The Advertiser,* November 4, 2013 [

http://www.adelaidenow.com.au/news/reynella-east-college-violent-porn-teacher-under-formal-investigation-from-teachers-registration-board/story-fni6uok5-1226752760141]; Jordanna Schriever and Sheradyn Holderhead, "South Australian Student Paid Hush Money after Being Wrongly Accused for Looking at Porn Says He Never Want [*sic*] Cash," *The Advertiser,* October 17, 2013 [Last accessed on 29 December 2014 at http://www.adelaidenow.com.au/news/south-australia/south-australian-student-paid-hush-money-after-being-wrongly-accused-for-looking-at-porn-says-he-never-want-cash/story-fni6uo1m-1226740812462?nk=71a922f348ef36eb34c674e98bd86d3b].

2.13. "Case Study: Pornography on a School Computer," New Zealand Teachers Council, [n.d.] [http://www.teacherscouncil.govt.nz/content/conduct-competence/case-studies/case-study-pornography-school-computer].

2.14. Imaeyen Ibanga, "Teacher: Wrong Computer Click Ruined My Life," *ABC News,* January 27, 2009 [http://abcnews.go.com/GMA/story?id=6739393].

2.15. *Id.*

2.16. Robert McMillan, "Teacher in Spyware Case Granted New Trial," *InfoWorld,* June 6, 2007 [http://www.infoworld.com/d/security-central/teacher-in-spyware-case-granted-new-trial-571].

2.17. Robert McMillan, "Spyware Case Finally Closed for Teacher Julie Amero," *Computerworld,* November 21, 2008 [http://www.computerworld.com/s/article/9121218/Spyware_c ase_finally_closed_for_teacher_Julie_Amero].

2.18. "The Zellner Affair," *MilwaukeeMag.com*, April 22, 2008 [http://www.milwaukeemag.com/article/242011-TheZellnerAffair].

2.19. *Id.*

3.1. Robert Quigley, "Today in History: The First Spam Email Ever Sent," Geekosystem.com, May 3, 2010 [Last accessed on 10 December 2014 at http://www.geekosystem.com/first-spam-email/].

3.2. Anick Jesdanun, "School Prank Starts 25 Years of Security Woes," Associated Press, September 1, 2007 [http://www.nbcnews.com/id/20534084/ns/technology_and_sc ience-security/t/school-prank-starts-years-security-woes/].

3.3. *Id.*

3.4. *The Economic Impact of Cybercrime and Cyberespionage.* Santa Clara: McAfee Center for Strategic and International Studies, July 2013. PDF. [http://www.mcafee.com/sg/resources/reports/rp-economic-impact-cybercrime.pdf].

3.5. Mike Frassinelli, "Teacher is charged as a stalker and a hacker," *The Star-Ledger*, January 15, 2008 [Last accessed on 10 December 2014 at http://www.nje3.org/index.php/teacher-is-charged-as-a-stalker-and-a-hacker]; Tom Quigley, "Teacher pleads guilty to harassing students, tapping into boy's AOL account," *The Express-Times*, May 8, 2008 [Last accessed on 10 December 2014 at http://blog.pennlive.com/lvbreakingnews/2008/05/teacher_ple ads_guilty_ot_haras.html].

3.6. Associated Press, "Steubenville official tried to cover up rape: court docs," *New York Post*, May 24, 2014 [Last accessed on 11 December 2014 at http://nypost.com/2014/05/24/steubenville-official-tried-to-cover-up-rape-court-docs/]; Associated Press, "Charges dropped for 2 school workers in rape case," KSNW-TV, July 2, 2014 [Last accessed on 11 December 2014 at http://ksn.com/2014/07/02/charges-dropped-for-2-school-workers-in-rape-case/].

3.7. Jimmie E. Gates, "Sager may be second to plead guilty in nursing home case,", *The Clarion-Ledger*, September 2, 2014 [Last accessed on 12 December 2014 at http://www.clarionledger.com/story/news/politics/2014/09/02 /another-defendant-may-plead-guilty-cochran-photo-case/14962995/]; "Guest says plea talks underway with Richard Sager," WAPT Jackson, October 9, 2014 [Last accessed on 12 December 2014 from http://www.wapt.com/news/central-mississippi/guest-says-plea-talks-underway-with-richard-sager/29030122].

3.8. Larry Lee, "Jailed Rhinelander Teacher Fired," WSAU, November 19, 2013 [Last accessed on 12 December

2014 from http://wsau.com/news/articles/2013/nov/19/jailed-rhinelander-teacher-fired/].

4.1. Danika Fears, "Oxford Dictionaries Names 'selfie' Word of the Year," *Today*, November 18, 2013 [http://www.today.com/news/oxford-dictionaries-names-selfie-word-year-2D11603600].

4.2. Eli Rosenberg, "In Weiner's Wake, a Brief History of the Word 'Sexting', *The Wire*, June 9, 2011 [http://www.thewire.com/national/2011/06/brief-history-sexting/38668/], *citing* Josey Vogels, "Textual Gratification: Quill or Keypad, It's All About Sex" *The Globe and Mail*, May 3, 2004 [http://www.theglobeandmail.com/technology/textual-gratification-quill-or-keypad-its-all-about-sex/article1136823/].

4.3. For a detailed explanation of how that happened, *see* Lane, Frederick S. *Obscene Profits: Entrepreneurs of Pornography in the Cyber Age: Entrepreneurs of Pornography in the Cyber Age*. New York: Routledge, 2000.

4.4. "Sex and Tech: Results from a Survey of Teens and Young Adults" The National Campaign to Prevent Teen and Unplanned Pregnancy and CosmoGirl.com, 2009 [http://www.thenationalcampaign.org/sextech/pdf/sextech_summary.pdf].

4.5. Mike Celizic, "Her Teen Committed Suicide over 'Sexting'," *Today*, March 6, 2009 [http://www.today.com/id/29546030#.UrnWy_RDutM].

4.6. Melissa Thomas, "Teen Hangs Herself after Harassment for a 'Sexting' Message, Parents Say," Courthouse News Service, December 7, 2009 [http://www.courthousenews.com/2009/12/07/Teen_Hangs_H erself_After_Harassment_For_a_Sexting_Message_Parents_ Say.htm].

4.7. Hutton, Thomas and Bailey, Kirk. *School Policies and Legal Issues Supporting Safe Schools*. Washington: Hamilton Fish Institute on School and Community Violence, George Washington University, 2008. Print.

4.8. Ting-Yi Oei, "My Students, My Cellphone, My Ordeal," *The Washington Post*, April 19, 2009 [http://articles.washingtonpost.com/2009-04-19/opinions/36879202_1_nude-pictures-cellphone-high-school-assistant].

4.9. *Id.*

4.10. *Id.*

4.11. *Id.*

4.12. http://www.urbandictionary.com/define.php?term=fl agging.

4.13. Ting-Yi Oei, "My Students, My Cellphone, My Ordeal," *The Washington Post*, April 19, 2009 [http://articles.washingtonpost.com/2009-04-

19/opinions/36879202_1_nude-pictures-cellphone-high-school-assistant].

4.14. Kim Zetter, "'Sexting' Hysteria Falsely Brands Educator as Child Pornographer," *Wired*, April 3, 2009 [http://www.wired.com/threatlevel/2009/04/sexting-hysteri/].

4.15. Michel Martin, "Asst. Principal Vindicated of 'Sexting' Charges, April 28, 2009 [http://www.npr.org/templates/story/story.php?storyId=10356 2915].

4.16. Kim Zetter, "'Sexting' Hysteria Falsely Brands Educator as Child Pornographer," *Wired*, April 3, 2009 [http://www.wired.com/threatlevel/2009/04/sexting-hysteri/].

4.17. Ting-Yi Oei, "My Students, My Cellphone, My Ordeal," *The Washington Post*, April 19, 2009 [http://articles.washingtonpost.com/2009-04-19/opinions/36879202_1_nude-pictures-cellphone-high-school-assistant].

5.1. There is a considerable debate among academics, researchers, and law enforcement about whether collection and consumption of child pornography inevitably leads to the sexual assault of children. This is not the place to either summarize or try to resolve that debate; there is an innate logic, however, to the argument that someone who works with children all day would be at greater risk of transitioning from passive consumption of child pornography to active assault.

5.2. 18 U.S.C. § 2256(8)(A). Subsections B and C prohibit computer-generated images of identifiable minors and modified images of identifiable minors, respectively.

5.3 18 U.S.C. § 2256(1).

5.4. "Micro Assists Child Porn Ring," *InfoWorld*, March 17, 1980, p. 1 [retrieved on 12 December 2014 from books.google.com].

5.5. *See, e.g.*, D'Vera Cohn, "Kiddy Porn Enters Computer Age," United Press International, December 8, 1982 [retrieved on 18 December 2008 from LexisNexis.com].

5.6. "Child Molesters Using Computer Diaries to Chronicle Their Exploits," Associated Press, February 17, 1984 [retrieved on 18 December 2008 from LexisNexis.com].

5.7. Larry Margasak, "Molesters Communicating Via Home Computers, FBI Says," Associated Press, June 11, 1985 [retrieved on 18 December 2008 from LexisNexis.com].

5.8. Tom Stanton, "Scanners Take Off," *PC Magazine*, October 13, 1987, pp. 185 *et seq.*.

5.9. Mitt Jones, "Nine Desktop Scanners that Do It All," *PC Magazine*, April 14, 1992, pp. 247 *et seq.*.

5.10. Bill Howard and Thom O'Connor, "Kodak DCS 420 Camera: Say Cheese and Forget About Film," *PC Magazine*, December 6, 1994, p. 40.

6.1. "1905 Teaching Contract for Story County, Iowa,&rdquo, Ames Historical Society, n.d. [http://www.ameshistory.org/contract.htm].

6.2. Harn Homestead 1889ers Museum, "One-Room Schoolhouse Teachers' Guide, n.d., p. 5.

6.3. *Id.*

6.4. Blount, Jackie M. *Destined to Rule the Schools: Women and the Superintendency, 1873-1995.* Albany: State University of New York Press, 1998. p. 93. Print.

6.5. *Id.*

6.6. "1900's: Supreme Court Decisions and Legislation," *The History of Women and Education,* National Women's History Museum, n.d. [http://www.nwhm.org/online-exhibits/education/1900s_3.htm].

6.7. Heather Clark, "Fired for Fornication: Teachers Sue Christian Schools Over Their Sexual Standards," *Christian News*, May 21, 2012 [http://christiannews.net/2012/05/21/fired-for-fornication-teachers-sue-christian-schools-over-their-sexual-standards/].

6.8. Warren Richey, "Florida teacher, fired for premarital sex, has right to a trial, court rules," *The Christian Sciene Monitor,* May 16, 2012 [http://www.csmonitor.com/USA/Justice/2012/0516/Florida-teacher-fired-for-premarital-sex-has-right-to-a-trial-court-rules].

6.9. Lisa Cornwell, "Jury finds for Cincinnati teacher fired from Catholic school while pregnant," *The Columbus Dispatch,* June 4, 2013 [http://www.dispatch.com/content/stories/local/2013/06/03/jury-finds-for-cincinnati-teacher-fired-while-pregnant.html].

6.10. Amanda Terkel, "Sen. Jim DeMint: Gays And Unmarried, Pregnant Women Should Not Teach Public School," *The Huffington Post,* October 2, 2010 [http://www.huffingtonpost.com/2010/10/02/demint-gays-unmarried-pregnant-women-teachers_n_748131.html].

6.11. Brittney R. Villalva, "Cathy Samford Fired by Christian School for Unmarried Pregnancy; Teacher Files Lawsuit," *The Christian Post,*April 12, 2012 [http://www.christianpost.com/news/cathy-samford-fired-for-unmarried-pregnancy-by-christian-school-teacher-files-lawsuit-73103/].

6.12. Heather Clark, "Fired for Fornication: Teachers Sue Christian Schools Over Their Sexual Standards," *Christian News,* May 21, 2012 [http://christiannews.net/2012/05/21/fired-for-fornication-teachers-sue-christian-schools-over-their-sexual-standards/].

7.1. Nancy White, "Cohasset school official resigns over 'snobby and arrogant' comments on Facebook," *The Patriot Ledger,* August 18, 2010 [http://www.patriotledger.com/topstories/x1104157578/Cohasset-school-administrator-resigns-over-snobby-and-arrogant-comments-on-Facebook].

7.2. *Id.*

7.3. Strauss, Emanuel. *Dictionary of European Proverbs* (Volume 2 ed.). Routledge (1994). p. 718.

7.4. Emil Protalinksi, "Teacher Should Be Fired for Facebook Comment, Judge Rules," *ZDNet,* November 15, 2011 [http://www.zdnet.com/blog/facebook/teacher-should-be-fired-for-facebook-comment-judge-rules/5375].

7.5. *Id.*

7.6. Chris Matyszczyk, "Teacher Accused of Mocking 7-year-old on Facebook," *CNET,* March 31, 2011 [http://news.cnet.com/8301-17852_3-20049480-71.html].

7.7. Cheryl Burton, "Teacher Allegedly Mocks Student on Facebook," *WLS-TV,* March 31, 2011 [http://abclocal.go.com/wls/story?id=8044485].

7.8. Chicago Public Schools Board of Education, "Warning Resolution—Dana Fitzpatrick," July 27, 2011 [http://www.cpsboe.org/content/actions/2011_07/11-0727-EX7.pdf].

7.9. Susan Edelman, "'I hate their guts—they are all devil's spawn," *New York Post*, February 5, 2012 [http://nypost.com/2012/02/05/i-hate-their-guts-they-are-all-devils-spawn/].

7.10. Susan Edelman, "Facebook ax upheld," *New York Post*, June 26, 2011 [http://nypost.com/2011/06/26/facebook-ax-upheld/].

7.11. Andy Newman, "Teacher's Facebook Post Didn't Warrant Firing, a Panel Upholds," *The New York Times*, May

8, 2013 [
http://www.nytimes.com/2013/05/09/nyregion/brooklyn-teacher-who-talked-out-of-school-can-keep-her-job.html].

8.1. "Columbus Teacher's Post-Election Facebook Post Leads To Investigation," WBNS-10TV, November 8, 2012 [Last accessed on 14 December 2014 at http://www.10tv.com/content/stories/2012/11/08/columbus-facebook-post-leads-to-teacher-investigation.html].

8.2. Steve Shaw, "OKC Teacher Under Fire Over Facebook Rant," News 9, November 7, 2012 [Last accessed on 14 December 2014 at http://www.news9.com/story/20036940/okc-teacher-under-fire-over-facebook-rant]; "Lamont Lowe, Oklahoma Teacher, Apologizes For Explosive, Hateful Post-Election Facebook Rant," *The Huffington Post*, November 8, 2012 [Last accessed on 14 December 2014 at http://www.huffingtonpost.com/2012/11/08/lamont-lowe-oklahoma-teac_n_2093153.html?utm_hp_ref=education].

8.3. Brendan James, "Texas 3rd-Grade Teacher Resigns After Wishing Ebola Would "Take Out Obama'," TPM.com, December 5, 2014 [Last accessed on 14 December 2014 at http://talkingpointsmemo.com/livewire/angela-box-texas-ebola-obama].

8.4. Ericka Mellon, "Teacher accused of anti-Muslim remarks to resign, get 3 months' pay," *Houston Chronicle*, December 4, 2014 [Last accessed on 14 December 2014 at http://www.chron.com/news/houston-texas/houston/article/Teacher-accused-of-anti-Muslim-remarks-to-resign-5934822.php].

8.5. Todd Unger, "Teacher placed on leave without pay over tweet," WFAA.com, November 10, 2014 [Last accessed on 15 December 2014 at http://www.wfaa.com/story/news/education/2014/11/09/racial-tweet-has-duncanville-teacher-in-twitter-storm/18784711/].

8.6. Robert Wilonsky, "Update: Duncanville ISD high school teacher resigns over "impulsive' tweet before school board can fire her," *The Dallas Morning News*, November 13, 2014 [Last accessed on 15 December 2014 at http://thescoopblog.dallasnews.com/2014/11/duncanville-isd-apologizes-for-high-school-teachers-reprehensible-offensive-tweet.html/].

8.7. "School board fires Texas teacher over Ferguson tweet," WFAA-TV, November 14, 2014 [Last accessed on 15 December 2014 at http://www.usatoday.com/story/news/nation/2014/11/14/texas-teacher-fired-ferguson-tweet/19020821/].

8.8. *Garcetti v. Ceballos*, 547 U.S. 410 (2006).

9.1. Maureen Downey, "Barrow teacher done in by anonymous 'parent' e-mail about her Facebook page," *Atlanta Journal-Constitution*, November 13, 2009 [http://blogs.ajc.com/get-schooled-blog/2009/11/13/barrow-teacher-done-in-by-anonymous-e-mail-with-perfect-punctuation/].

9.2. *Id.*

9.3. *Id.*

9.4. Deanna Allen, "Former Apalachee Teacher Appealing Decision in Facebook Lawsuit," *Barrow Patch,* May 6, 2013 [http://barrow.patch.com/groups/editors-picks/p/former-apalachee-teacher-appealing-decision-in-facebook-lawsuit].

9.5. Snejana Farberov, "High school teacher, 23, 'tweeted nude photos of herself, called her students JAIL BAIT and talked about getting high'," *Daily Mail,* January 30, 2013 [http://www.dailymail.co.uk/news/article-2270383/Carly-McKinney-High-school-teacher-23-tweeted-nude-photos-called-students-JAIL-BAIT-talked-getting-high.html].

9.6. *Urban Dictionary*, s.v. "crunk."

9.7. *Urban Dictionary*, s.v. "framp stamp."

9.8. Ryan Broderick, "Half-Naked Photos, Pot-Smoking Tweets Get Teacher Suspended," *BuzzFeed,* January 30, 2013 [http://www.buzzfeed.com/ryanhatesthis/worlds-dumbest-teacher-tweets-photos-of-herself-h].

9.9. "'Carly Crunk Bear' teacher Carly McKinney no longer part of school district," *WTSP.com,* March 26, 2013 [http://www.wtsp.com/news/local/story.aspx?storyid=307185].

9.10. Matt Ferner, "#FreeCrunkBear: Carly McKinney, High School Teacher Who Tweeted Semi-Nude Pics, Backed By Her Students On Twitter," *The Huffington Post,* January 30, 2013 [http://www.huffingtonpost.com/2013/01/31/freecrunkbear-carly-mckin_n_2586352.html].

9.11. "Settlement Reached in Teacher's Stripper Photo Suspension," *WPXI*, August 17, 2010 [http://www.wpxi.com/news/news/settlement-reached-in-teachers-stripper-photo-susp/nGrRS/].

10.1. "Give me a 'Why?' Cheerleading coach fired after 'angry email campaign from a parent upset she worked at Hooters,'" *Daily Mail*, December 8, 2011.

10.2. Susan Hatch, "Amy Adams Once a Hooters Waitress - Now Cheerleading Coach is Famous for Job, Too," *National Ledger*, March 26, 2012 [Last accessed on 15 December 2014 at http://www.nationalledger.com/pop-culture-news/amy-adams-once-a-hooters-waitress-270704.shtml#.VI-RTtXF_P8].

10.3. "Give me a 'Why?' Cheerleading coach fired after 'angry email campaign from a parent upset she worked at Hooters,'" *Daily Mail*, December 8, 2011.

10.4. Jake Nordbye, "Hooters waitress gains national spotlight after firing as Estero cheerleading coach," *The Banner*, March 9, 2012 [Last accessed on 15 December 2014 at http://www.naplesnews.com/community/bonita-banner/hooters-waitress-fired-cheerleading-coach-estero].

10.5. Zoe Mintz, "Olivia Sprauer, Florida Teacher Fired For Sexy Bikini Photos, Victoria Valentine James Alter-Ego Revealed," *International Business Times*, May 9, 2013 [Last accessed on 15 December 2014 at http://www.ibtimes.com/olivia-sprauer-florida-teacher-fired-sexy-bikini-photos-victoria-valentine-james-alter-ego-revealed].

10.6. "Video: Florida Teacher Fired Over Modeling In Bikini Photos Online," Fox2Now.com, May 10, 2013 [Last accessed on 15 December 2014 at http://fox2now.com/2013/05/10/florida-teacher-fired-over-modeling-in-bikini-photos-online/].

10.7. David Schoetz, "Teacher Moonlighting as Bikini Mate Cut Loose," *ABC News,* April 30, 2008 [http://abcnews.go.com/US/story?id=4756166].

10.8. *Id.*

10.9. Susan Edelman, "Manhattan HS guidance counselor stripped of job over steamy-photo past," *New York Post,* October 7, 2012 [Last accessed on 15 December 2014 at http://nypost.com/2012/10/07/manhattan-hs-guidance-counselor-stripped-of-job-over-steamy-photo-past/].

10.10. *Id.*

10.11. *Id.*

10.12. Adam Klasfeld, "Fired Teacher Says NYC Schools Had a Tizzy," *Courthouse News Service*, March 23, 2012 [Last accessed on 15 December 2014 at http://www.courthousenews.com/2012/03/23/44953.htm].

10.13. Decision and Order, *Tiffani Notre Ellis v. The Department of Education of the City of New York and The City School District of the City of New York*, Index No.: 500554/2012, July 3, 2012 [Last accessed on 15 December

2014 at https://cases.justia.com/new-york/other-courts/2013-ny-slip-op-32158-u.pdf?ts=1379432116].

11.1. Chris Monty, "Crystal Defanti Video Scandal," *Blippitt.com,* July 3, 2009 [http://www.blippitt.com/crystal-defanti-video-scandal-video/].

11.2. Leslie H. Dixon, "Oxford Hills football coach resigns after allegedly posting nude photo on Facebook," *Bangor Daily News,* February 13, 2012 [http://bangordailynews.com/2012/02/13/news/lewiston-auburn/oxford-hills-football-coach-resigns-after-allegedly-posting-inappropriate-photo-on-facebook/].

11.3. Leslie H. Dixon, "Oxford Hills Football Coach Resigns after Allegedly Posting Nude Photo on Facebook," *Bangor Daily News*, February 13, 2012.

11.4. Chris Monty, "Crystal Defanti Video Scandal," *Blippitt.com,* July 3, 2009 [http://www.blippitt.com/crystal-defanti-video-scandal-video/].

11.5. *Id.*

11.6. David Begnaud, "Teacher Gives Sex DVD to Students," *CBS13,* July 1, 2009 [http://cbs13.com/local/teacher.porn.dvd.2.1068250.html].

11.7. Maxim Alter and Holly Pennebaker, "Cincinnati Hills Christian Academy Teacher Resigns After Nude Photo Spread Online," *WCPO*, December 4, 2013 [http://www.wcpo.com/news/local-news/cincinnati-hills-christian-academy-fifth-grade-teacher-put-on-leave-over-nude-photo-online].

11.8. Maxim Alter, "Man behind 'revenge porn' website with Cincinnati teacher's nude photo arrested," *WCPO*, December 11, 2013 [http://www.wcpo.com/news/local-news/man-behind-revenge-porn-website-with-cincinnati-teachers-nude-photo-arrested].

11.9. David Gardner, "Elementary school teacher fired after homemade sex tape was sent to parents," *Daily Mail*, September 23, 2011 [http://www.dailymail.co.uk/news/article-2041189/Natalie-Santagata-Teacher-fired-sex-tape-sent-parents-Facebook.html].

11.10. "Teacher fired after racy photos, video surface," *WBBH*, September 22, 2011 [http://www.nbc-2.com/story/15529519/2011/09/22/teacher-fired-after-racy-photos-video-surface].

12.1. andrewj54, "MA-SEN: Scott Brown Posed Nude," DailyKos.com, January 10, 2010 [Last accessed on 16 December 2014 at http://www.dailykos.com/story/2010/01/10/823549/-MA-Sen-160-Scott-Brown-posed-nude].

12.2. *The People v. Harold Freeman*, 46 Cal. 3d 419; 758 P.2d 1128; 250 Cal. Rptr. 598 (Calif. 1988).

12.3. Google, "Company Overview," n.d. (Last accessed January 4, 2014) [http://www.google.com/about/company/].

12.4. Lee Moran, "Texas high school teacher who posed for Playboy under fire after starring as 'Coed of the Month'," *New York Daily News*, October 8, 2013 [Last accessed on 16 December 2014 from http://www.nydailynews.com/news/national/texas-high-school-teacher-posed-playboy-coed-month-article-1.1479224].

12.5. Nadine DeNinno, "Cristy Nicole Deweese: Meet The Former Nude Playboy Model Turned High School Spanish Teacher Outraging Parents," *International Business Times*, October 8, 2013 [http://www.ibtimes.com/cristy-nicole-deweese-meet-former-nude-playboy-model-turned-high-school-spanish-teacher-outraging].

12.6. Tawnell Hobbs, "Dallas ISD Teacher Who Posed Naked on Playboy's Website Causing a Stir," October 4, 2013 [http://educationblog.dallasnews.com/2013/10/dallas-isd-teacher-who-posed-naked-on-playboys-website-causing-a-stir.html/].

12.7. Eric Nicholson, "Dallas ISD Has Reportedly Fired Cristy Nicole Deweese, its Spanish-Teaching Playboy Model," *Dallas Observer,* October 14, 2013 [http://blogs.dallasobserver.com/unfairpark/2013/10/dallas_isd_reportedly_fired_cr.php].

12.8. "A Cautionary Tale," *Kentucky School News and Commentary*, March 9, 2011 [Last accessed on 16 December 2014 at http://theprincipal.blogspot.com/2011/03/cautionary-tale.html]; "Teacher Troubles," Dr. Phil.com, December 6,

2006 [Last accessed on 16 December 2014 at http://drphil.com/shows/show/805/].

12.9. "Teacher's appeal withdrawn in lawsuit: Former Reidland High School teacher Tericka Dye has a new teaching job out of state," *The Paducah Sun*, February 13, 2007 [Last accessed on 16 December 2014 at http://cloud-computing.tmcnet.com/news/2007/02/13/2333139.htm].

12.10. Kate Sheehy, "Hot for Teacher," *New York Post*, March 9, 2011 [Last accessed on 5 September 2014 at http://nypost.com/2011/03/09/hot-for-teacher/].

12.11. Laura Hibbard, "Kevin Hogan, Boston High School Teacher, On Leave After Starring In Pornographic Films," November 30, 2011 [Last accessed on 16 December 2014 at http://www.huffingtonpost.com/2011/11/30/kevin-hogan-high-school-t_n_1121376.html].

12.12. "Teacher who starred in porn no longer at school," MyFoxBoston.com, July 25, 2012 [Last accessed on 16 December 2014 at http://www.myfoxboston.com/story/19114748/2012/07/25/teacher-who-starred-in-porn-no-longer-at-school].

12.13. "Miami-Dade teacher Shawn Loftis fired for porn past," WTSP.com, August 30, 2011 [last access on 16 December 2014 at http://www.wtsp.com/news/article/208109/11/Miami-Dade-teacher-Shawn-Loftis-fired-for-porn-past].

12.14. Michael Sheridan, "Florida teacher, Shawn Loftis, with gay porn past gets job back," *New York Daily News*,

March 11, 2012 [Last accessed on 16 December 2014 at http://www.nydailynews.com/news/national/florida-teacher-shawn-loftis-gay-porn-job-back-article-1.1037132].

12.15. Gus Garcia-Roberts, "Ex-Porn Star Shawn Loftis On Miami-Dade Schools Refusing to Reinstate Him: 'They're Going to Have a Lawsuit On Their F*#king Hands'," *Miami New Times*, March 13, 2012 [Last accessed on 16 December 2014 at http://blogs.miaminewtimes.com/riptide/2012/03/ex-porn_star_shawn_loftis_on_m.php].

12.16. "Playboy Photos Future For Tiffany Shepherd, Bikini Teacher Turned Down," *The Post Chronicle*, November 1, 2008 [http://www.postchronicle.com/cgi-bin/artman/exec/view.cgi?archive=104&num=182962].

12.17. Eitan Gavish, "Bikini-Clad Teacher Tiffany Shepherd Turns to Porn after Being Fired from Florida High School," *New York Daily News,* August 21, 2009 [http://www.nydailynews.com/news/national/bikini-clad-teacher-tiffany-shepherd-turns-porn-fired-florida-high-school-article-1.397203].

12.18. "Bikini Teacher," *Palm Beach Post*, November 27, 2014 [Last accessed on 17 December 2014 at http://www.palmbeachpost.com/gallery/news/local/bikini-teacher/gHJd/].

12.19. *Id.*

13.1. Rudyard Kipling, "On the City Wall," from *Indian Tales*(1888), *The Literature Network* [http://www.online-literature.com/kipling/indian-tales/13/].

13.2. Corina Vanek, "Former Phoenix teacher sentenced in prostitution sting," *The Republic*, June 4, 2014 [Last accessed on 17 December 2014 at http://www.azcentral.com/story/news/local/phoenix/2014/06/04/phoenix-teacher-prostitution-sting-sentencing-abrk/9966805/].

13.3. Brittany Schmidt, "Former La Crosse teacher arrested in Winona prostitution sting," News8000.com, August 6, 2014 [Last accessed on 17 December 2014 at http://www.news8000.com/news/former-la-crosse-teacher-nabbed-in-winona-prostitution-sting/26752784].

13.4. Bea Chang, "Teacher in Texas Arrested for Prostitution," KARE11.com, August 19, 2008 [Last accessed on 16 December 2013 at http://www.kare11.com/news/article/522349/18/Teacher-in-Texas-arrested-for-prostitution].

13.5. Alex Wukman, "Teacher accused of prostitution resigns," *Cleveland Advocate*, November 21, 2010 [Last accessed on 17 December 2014 at http://www.yourhoustonnews.com/cleveland/news/teacher-accused-of-prostitution-resigns/article_be406ebc-e621-555d-8d97-3635b20097fc.html?mode=jqm].

13.6. Cindy Horswell, "Cleveland teacher on leave after prostitution charge," *Houston Chronicle*, August 19, 2008 [

Last accessed on 17 December 2014 at
http://www.chron.com/news/houston-texas/article/Cleveland-
teacher-on-leave-after-prostitution-1654431.php].

13.7. Dave Weber, "Seminole Teacher Resigns Over
Brothel Visits," *Orlando Sentinel,* December 11, 2012 [
http://articles.orlandosentinel.com/2012-12-11/features/os-
seminole-brothel-teacher-20121211_1_seminole-teacher-ron-
pinnell-chemistry-teacher].

13.8. "Police: Teacher Used School Computer to Meet
Prostitutes," *WESH,* November 15, 2012 [
http://www.wesh.com/news/central-florida/Police-Teacher-
used-school-computer-to-meet-prostitutes/-
/11788162/17428790/-/10iw5fjz/-/index.html].

13.9. Holly Zachariah, "Deputies Say Teacher Who
Skipped Class Went to Motel to Work as Prostitute," *The
Columbus Dispatch,* February 11, 2009 [
http://www.dispatch.com/content/stories/local/2009/02/11/lct
each.html].

13.10. Holly Zachariah, "Teacher Accused of Prostitution
Won't Resign," *The Columbus Dispatch,* February 13, 2009 [
http://www.dispatch.com/content/stories/local/2009/02/13/tea
cherbust.html].

13.11. "Teacher Accused of Prostitution," *The
CantonRep,* February 21, 2009 [
http://www.cantonrep.com/x426337949/Teacher-accused-of-
prostitution-resigns?photo=0].

13.12. "Former Teacher Pleads Guilty After Ditching Class for Sex," *KTVO-TV,* March 4, 2009 [http://www.heartlandconnection.com/news/story.aspx?id=268 396#.UshMf_RDutM].

13.13. "Little Rock Teacher Resigns After Pleading Guilty to Prostitution," *Fox News,* February 19, 2011 [http://www.foxnews.com/us/2011/02/19/little-rock-teacher-resigns-pleading-guilty-prostitution/?test=latestnews].

13.14. "Solona Islam Resigns after the Little Rock School District Learns of Her 2010 Prostitution Conviction," *KTHV,* February 18, 2011 [http://origin.todaysthv.com/news/local/story.aspx?storyid=14 4127].

13.15. Meredith Jessup, "Arkansas Teacher Put on Paid Leave Following Prostitution Conviction," *TheBlaze.com,* February 19, 2011 [http://www.theblaze.com/stories/2011/02/19/arkansas-teacher-put-on-paid-leave-following-prostitution-conviction/].

13.16. Melissa Petro, "Thoughts From a Former Craigslist Sex Worker," HuffingtonPost.com, September 7, 2010 [Last accessed on 19 May 2011 at http://www.huffingtonpost.com/melissa-petro/post_803_b_707975.html].

13.17. Sharon Otterman, "Teacher with Sex-Worker Past Resigns,", *New York Times,* January 21, 2011 [Last accessed on 17 December 2014 at http://cityroom.blogs.nytimes.com/2011/01/21/teacher-with-sex-worker-past-resigns/].

13.18. Elizabeth Dwoskin, "Melissa Petro Gives Up Her Fight to be a Teacher after Prostitution Revelation," *The Village Voice*, February 10, 2011 [Last accessed on 17 December 2014 at http://blogs.villagevoice.com/runninscared/2011/02/melissa_petro_g.php].

14.1. Sherry Posnick-Goodwin, "Cyberbullying of Teachers," *California Educator*, March 2012 [Last accessed on 19 December 2014 at http://www.cta.org/Professional-Development/Publications/2012/03/March-Educator-2012/Cyberbullying-of-teachers.aspx].

14.2. Caleb Garling, "Study: 26 percent of teachers cite cyberbullying by parents," Yahoo! News, August 16, 2011 [Last accessed on 19 December 2014 at http://news.yahoo.com/study-26-percent-teachers-cite-cyberbullying-parents-211206855.html].

14.3. Richard Garner, "Teachers: 'Our pupils are targeting us on social media' with more than a quarter victims of abuse," *The Independent*, April 21, 2014 [Last accessed on 19 December 2014 at http://www.independent.co.uk/news/uk/home-news/teachers-our-pupils-are-targeting-uswith-more-than-a-quarter-victims-of-abuse-on-social-media-9272462.html].

14.4. *Id.*

14.5. Lisa Miller, "Cyberbullying Law Shields Teachers From Student Tormentors," National Public Radio, February 19, 2013 [Last accessed on 18 December 2014 at http://www.npr.org/2013/02/19/172329526/cyber-bulling-law-shields-teachers-from-student-tormentors].

14.6. Claude Carroué, "UK Teacher' Union Takes on Cyberbullying," United4Education.org, n.d. [Last accessed on 20 December 2014 at http://www.unite4education.org/uncategorized/uk-teachers-union-takes-on-cyberbullying/].

14.7. As someone who has worked in field of computer forensics for more than fifteen years, I can attest that it is more difficult than people realize to achieve true anonymity online. But in the case of most online bullying, the time and effort required to ferret out the people responsible is much greater than the actual harm caused by the bullying.

14.8. *Urban Dictionary*, s.v. "cyberbaiting."

14.9. "Surprising Findings," Norton Online Family Report 2011," Symantec.com, 2011 [Last accessed on 20 December 2014 at http://www.symantec.com/content/en/us/home_homeoffice/html/cybercrimereport/].

14.10. Susan Donaldson James, "Cyberbaiting on the Rise as Teacher Tantrums Posted to YouTube," ABC News, January 4, 2011 [Last accessed on 20 December 2014 at http://abcnews.go.com/Health/cyberbaiting-rise-teacher-tantrums-posted-youtube/story?id=15282396].

14.11. *Id.*

15.1. Michael Maslin, "Peter Steiner on the 20th Anniversary of 'On the Internet, nobody knows you're a dog.'" Ink Spill, July 5, 2013 [Last accessed on 20 December 2014 at http://michaelmaslin.com/inkspill/peter-steiner-20th-anniversary-on-internet-nobody-knows-youre-dog-2/].

15.2. Todd Ruger, "MySpace Creeping into School Space," *The Herald-Tribune*, April 5, 2006 [Last accessed on April 22, 2006 at http://www.heraldtribune.com/apps/pbcs.dll/article?AID=/20060405/NEWS/604050595].

15.3. Associated Press, "Authorities Blame 8th Grader for Web Hoax," WCCO.com, April 22, 2006 [Last accessed on April 22, 2006 at http://wcco.com/topstories/local_story_112160715.html].

15.4. Chris Cox, Facebook.com Blog, October 1, 2014 [Last accessed on 21 December 2014 at https://www.facebook.com/chris.cox/posts/10101301777354543]. Cox's post was in response to a controversy that arose over whether drag queens could create Facebook user accounts and pages under their adopted names. Vindu Goel, "Facebook to Ease Policies on Using Real Names for Accounts," *New York Times*, October 1, 2014 [Last accessed on 21 December 2014 at http://bits.blogs.nytimes.com/2014/10/01/facebook-agrees-to-ease-rules-on-real-names/].

15.5. "Student suspended for faking teacher's Facebook page," CBC.ca, May 18, 2011 [Last accessed on 21 December 2014 at http://www.cbc.ca/news/canada/prince-edward-island/student-suspended-for-faking-teacher-s-facebook-page-1.1093339].

15.6. David Kravets, "Student Who Created Facebook Group Critical of Teacher Sues High School Over Suspension," *Wired*, December 9, 2008 [Last accessed on 21 December 2014 at http://www.wired.com/2008/12/us-student-inte/].

15.7. "Student Suspended For Facebook Page Gets $15K In Settlement," CBS Miami, December 29, 2010 [Last accessed on 21 December 2014 at http://miami.cbslocal.com/2010/12/29/student-suspended-for-facebook-page-gets-15k-in-settlement/].

15.8. "Georgia Court Rules Parents May Be Liable for Child's Fake Facebook Account," Bloomberg BNA, October 22, 2014 [Last accessed on 21 December 2014 at http://www.bna.com/georgia-court-rules-n17179906173/].

15.9. Mike Flacy, "Principal resigns after creating fake Facebook profile to spy on students," Digital Trends, May 7, 2012 [Last accessed on 21 December 2014 at http://www.digitaltrends.com/social-media/principal-resigns-after-creating-fake-facebook-profile-to-spy-on-students/]; Kim Zetter, "Principal Accused of Spying on Students, Parents With Fake Facebook Account," *Wired*, May 8, 2012 [Last access on 21 December 2014 at http://www.wired.com/2012/05/principal-spying-on-students/all/].

15.10. Molly Walsh, "Facebook Snooping Nets Second Athlete," *Burlington Free Press*, January 13, 2008 [Last accessed on 13 January 2008 at http://www.burlingtonfreepress.com/apps/pbcs.dll/article?AID=/20080113/NEWS02/801130322/1007].

15.11. Bob Cook, "High School Coaches Targeted by Fake Twitter Accounts," *Forbes*, January 20, 2012 [Last access on 21 December 2014 at http://www.forbes.com/sites/bobcook/2012/01/20/high-school-coaches-targeted-by-fake-twitter-accounts/].

16.1. "Overview | State Statutes | Cyberbullying," National Conference of State Legislatures, December 5, 2013 [Last accessed on 19 December 2013 at http://www.ncsl.org/research/telecommunications-and-information-technology/cyberstalking-and-cyberharassment-laws.aspx].

16.2. Jeff Mitchell, "Timber Creek High math teacher charged with harassment of 17-year-old girl," *South Jersey Times,*, July 12, 2013 [Last accessed on 25 December 2014 at http://www.nj.com/camden/index.ssf/2013/07/timber_creek_high_math_teacher_charged_with_harassment_of_17-year-old_girl.html]; Phil Dunn, "Upheld: Teacher's firing for inappropriate texts to students," *Courier-Post*, August 29, 2014 [Last accessed on 25 December 2014 at http://www.courierpostonline.com/story/news/local/south-jersey/2014/08/29/upheld-teachers-firing-inappropriate-texts-students/14816109/].

16.3. Jason Frazer and Rob Polansky, "'Teacher of the year' accused of harassing teen through social media," WFSB.com, May 22, 2014 [Last accessed on 25 December 2014 at http://www.wfsb.com/story/25587628/woman-goes-from-teacher-of-the-year-to-suspect-in-a-crime].

16.4. "North Branford Teacher Pleads Not Guilty to Harassing Teen on Social Media Site," NBC Connecticut, May 29, 2014 [Last accessed on 25 December 2014 at http://www.nbcconnecticut.com/news/local/Stephanie-DeFrance-Arrest-Teacher-North-Branford-Totoket-Elementary-TVES-Middletown-260194731.html].

16.5. Lauren O'Neill, "Teen arrested for harassing teacher with 'cyberbullying app' Streetchat," CBC News, October 6, 2014 [Last accessed on 19 December 2014 at http://www.cbc.ca/newsblogs/yourcommunity/2014/10/teen-arrested-for-harassing-teacher-with-cyberbullying-app-streetchat.html]

16.6. "Overview | State Statutes | Cyberbullying," National Conference of State Legislatures, December 5, 2013 [Last accessed on 19 December 2013 at http://www.ncsl.org/research/telecommunications-and-information-technology/cyberstalking-and-cyberharassment-laws.aspx].

16.7. N.C. Gen. Stat. § 14-196.3(b)(3).

16.8. "South Charlotte Teen Charged With Cyberstalking Of Teacher," WSOCTV.com, January 31, 2008 [Last accessed on December 21, 2010 at http://www.wsoctv.com/news/15186700/detail.html].

16.9. Reshma Kirpalani, "Teacher Charged With Cyberstalking Roils North Carolina Town," ABC News, June 25, 2011 [Last accessed on 26 December 2014 at http://abcnews.go.com/US/teacher-charged-cyberstalking-students/story?id=13923107&singlePage=true].

16.10. Marissa Jasek, "FIRST ON 3: Pender Co. teacher apologizes for inappropriate texts to student, reaches plea deal," WWAY.com, July 21, 2011 [Last accessed on 26 December 2014 at http://www.wwaytv3.com/2011/07/21/first-3-pender-co-teacher-apologizes-for-inappropriate-texts-to-student-reaches-plea-deal].

16.11. "Revoked License," North Carolina State Board of Education, n.d. [Last accessed on 26 December 2014 at http://stateboard.ncpublicschools.gov/legal-affairs/disciplinary-process/revoked-license].

16.12. Chris Foreman, "Suspended Penn-Trafford teacher charged with stalking student," TribLive.com, July 25, 2014 [Last accessed on 26 December 2014 at http://triblive.com/neighborhoods/yourpenntrafford/yourpenn traffordmore/6505464-74/garet-student-complaint#axzz3MwVspnTv].

16.13. *Id.*

17.1 "Band Teacher Surrenders at St. Johns County Jail," WJXT.com, March 15, 2006 [Last accessed on 13 March 2006 at http://www.news4jax.com/news/7967117/detail.html?subid= 22100425&qs=1;bp=t].

17.2 "Former Castleton Teacher Set for Video Voyeurism Hearing," *Times-News*, December 7, 2011 [Last accessed on 12 December 2011 at http://magicvalley.com/news/local/education/former-castleford-teacher-set-for-video-voyeurism-hearing/article_850337dc-3df8-527e-8f84-e325bfb1cac4.html].

17.3 Josh Poland, "Former School Theater Instructor Sentenced To 4 Years On Voyeurism Charges," August 15, 2013 [Last accessed on 16 August 2013 at http://www.10tv.com/content/stories/2013/08/15/columbus-former-theater-teacher-sentenced-for-voyeurism.html].

17.4 "Former Teacher Pleads Guilty to Voyeurism," WLFI.com, April 8, 2014 [Last accessed on 23 December 2014 at http://wlfi.com/2014/04/08/former-teacher-pleads-guilty-to-voyeurism/].

17.5 "Music Teacher Charged in Child Porn Case," AP Wire Service, March 13, 2001 [Last accessed on March 20, 2001 at http://newsfinder.arinet.com/fpweb/fp.dll/$stargeneral/htm/x_dv.htm/_ibyx/cg03026/_itox/starnet/_svc/news/_Id/70751532 8/_k/qKaNfSEInvTFmUfX]; Al Baker, "Man Accused in

Cheerleader Video Voyeur Case," *New York Times*, April 4, 2001 [Last accessed on March 23, 2013 at http://www.nytimes.com/2001/04/04/nyregion/man-accused-in-cheerleader-voyeur-video-case.html].

17.6 "CreepShots... where the camera captures for eternity, what the eye sees for only moments," MetaReddit.com, n.d. [Last accessed on 24 December 2014 at http://metareddit.com/r/CreepShots].

17.7 Nina Golgowski, "High school teacher fired for posting pictures of his underage female students on 'Creepshot' website," *Daily Mail*, September 27, 2012 [Last accessed on 24 December 2014 at http://www.dailymail.co.uk/news/article-2209611/Creepshot-East-Coweta-teacher-fired-posting-pictures-underage-female-students-Reddit.html]. We'll put aside for the moment the myriad issues raised by the fact that there is nothing that prevents high school students—or even younger children—from viewing sites like Creepshots.

17.8 A copy of Weagleweaglewde's Reddit comments can be viewed on Imgr.com at http://i.imgur.com/tXBtM.png.

17.9 Ben Nelms, "Coweta teacher fired for posting pics of students on Creepshots," TheCitizen.com, September 28, 2012 [Last accessed on 24 December 2014 at http://www.thecitizen.com/articles/09-28-2012/coweta-teacher-fired-posting-pics-students-creepshots].

17.10 18 U.S.C. § 2256(2)(A). Most state child pornography statutes contain similar language that arguably encompasses photos of clothed children.

17.11 "Teacher had 16,000 indecent images,", BBC, April 14, 2014 [Last accessed on 25 December 2014 at http://www.bbc.com/news/uk-wales-26953879]; "Voyeur teacher Gareth Williams jailed for five years," BBC, May 14, 2014 [Last accessed on 25 December 2014 at http://www.bbc.com/news/uk-wales-south-east-wales-27468470].

17.12 "Prosecutors: Former McLoud Teacher Recorded Video Of Naked Students In Classroom," News9.com, December 15, 2011 [Last accessed on 14 December 2014 from http://www.news9.com/story/16330521/former-mcloud-teacher-due-in-court-thursday]; "Prosecutor: Okla. 3rd grade teacher took pictures, video of naked female students," CBS News, December 15, 2011 [Last accessed on 14 December 2014 at http://www.cbsnews.com/news/prosecutor-okla-3rd-grade-teacher-took-pictures-video-of-naked-female-students/]; Andrew Knittle, "Former Oklahoma teacher, former professor enter pleas to sex crimes against children," NewsOK, January 9, 2013 [Last accessed on 14 December 2014 at http://newsok.com/former-oklahoma-teacher-former-professor-enter-pleas-to-sex-crimes-against-children/article/3744464]; "McLoud Teacher Who Admitted Taking Explicit Pictures Of Students Asks For Probation," NewsOn6.com, March 11, 2013 [Last accessed on 14 December 2014 at http://www.newson6.com/story/21579107/mcloud-teacher-who-admitted-taking-explicit-pictures-of-students-asks-for-probation]; "Kimberly Crain changes plea, sentenced," KOCO.com, March 22, 2013 [Last accessed on 14 December 2014 at http://www.koco.com/news/oklahomanews/around-oklahoma/Kimberly-Crain-changes-plea-sentenced/19429112#ixzz3DLztTeGl].

17.13 Elaine Van Develde, "Colleagues Are Stunned by Child Porn Charges," Atlanticville.com, September 3, 2004 [Last accessed on 8 December 2013 at http://atl.gmnews.com/news/2004-09-03/Front_page/021.html]; Joe Ryan, "Ex-math teacher admits distributing child pornography," *The Star-Ledger*, June 4, 2008 [Last accessed on 25 December 2014 at http://www.nj.com/news/index.ssf/2008/06/exmath_teacher_a dmits_distribu.html].

17.14 John Curran, "Seven New Sex Charges Against Former Bradford Teacher," Associated Press, December 21, 2007 [Last accessed on 21 December 2007 at http://www.boston.com/news/local/vermont/articles/2007/12/ 21/seven_new_sex_charges_against_former_bradford_teache r/]; "Bradford Teacher Sentenced to 25 Years for Producing Child Pornography," U.S. Attorney's Office, March 18, 2009 [Last accessed on 25 December 2014 at http://www.fbi.gov/albany/press-releases/2009/alfo031809.htm].

17.15 Alexandra Klein, "Former D.C. teacher makes FBI "Most Wanted" list after 2008 child porn

discovery, *Washington Post*, May 17, 2012 [Last accessed on
18 May 2012 at
http://www.washingtonpost.com/local/crime/former-dc-
teacher-makes-fbi-most-wanted-list-after-2008-child-porn-
discovery/2012/05/16/gIQAPJJHUU_story.html]; Allison
Klein, "Ex-Beauvoir teacher Eric Toth, wanted on child
pornography charges, is found abroad," *Washington Post*,
April 22, 2013 [Last accessed on 25 December 2014 at
http://www.washingtonpost.com/local/2013/04/22/fc70abbe-
ab75-11e2-b6fd-ba6f5f26d70e_story.html].

17.16 Daniel Marin, "Prosecutor: Irvin High Dance
Teacher Made Child Porn In His Home, May Have Up To 70
Victims," KVIA.com, September 30, 2010 [Last accessed on
25 December 2014 at http://www.kvia.com/news/Prosecutor-
Irvin-High-Dance-Teacher-Made-Child-Porn-In-His-Home-
May-Have-Up-To-70-Victims/544198]; Eleana Arteaga,
"Ex-Irvin High Teacher Marco Alferez Sentenced to Max.
Term in Prison for Child Porn," KTSM.com, January 12,
2012 [Last accessed on 25 December 2014 at
http://www.ktsm.com/news/ex-irvin-high-teacher-marco-
alferez-sentenced-to-max-term-in-prison-for-child-porn].

17.17 "Ex-Stoneham school official charged with child
porn kills self," WCVB.com, December 17, 2014 [Last
accessed on 25 December 2014 at
http://www.wcvb.com/news/exstoneham-school-official-
charged-with-child-porn-kills-self/30240262].

18.1 *See, e.g.*, Theresa Seiger, "Family of boy sexually abused by teacher at Mary G. Montgomery grappling with after-effects of abuse," AL.com, January 16, 2014 [Last accessed on 26 December 2014 at http://blog.al.com/live/2014/01/family_of_boy_sexually_abused.html].

18.2 Brendan Kirby, "Mobile County grand jury indicts Mary Montgomery teacher accused of having sex with student," AL.com, April 14, 2013 [Last accessed on 26 December 2014 at http://blog.al.com/live/2013/04/mobile_county_grand_jury_indic_2.html].

18.3 Paul Thompson, "Married math teacher, 28, is indicted on sodomy charges after 'oral sex with 14-year-old male student,' *The Daily Mail*, April 15, 2013 [Last accessed on 26 December 2014 at http://www.dailymail.co.uk/news/article-2309461/Alicia-Gray-charges-Married-math-teacher-28-indicted-sex-charges-oral-sex-14-year-old-male-student.html].

18.4 Theresa Seiger, "Semmes high school teacher turns herself in as investigation into alleged student-teacher relationship continues," AL.com, February 25, 2013 [Last accessed on 26 December 2014 at http://blog.al.com/live/2013/02/semmes_high_school_teacher_tur.html].

18.5 Michael Dumas, "Former Mobile County teacher pleads guilty to sex abuse with student, surrenders teaching certificate," AL.com, January 10, 2014 [Last accessed on 26 December 2014 at http://blog.al.com/live/2014/01/former_mobile_county_teach er_p.html].

18.6 Gemma Mullin, "Married teaching assistant, 32, sent thousands of lewd texts after starting two-year affair with 14-year-old schoolboy - and threatened suicide when his parents found out," *The Daily Mail*, October 13, 2014 [Last accessed on 26 December 2014 at http://www.dailymail.co.uk/news/article-2791114/teaching-assistant-sent-thousands-texts-starting-two-year-affair-14-year-old-schoolboy.html].

18.7 Olivia-Anne Cleary, "Female teacher who had 2-year affair with 14-year-old student is spared jail," Daily.co.uk, October 14, 2014 [Last accessed on 26 December 2014 at http://www.bestdaily.co.uk/your-life/news/a603479/female-teacher-who-had-2-year-affair-with-14-year-old-student-is-spared-jail.html].

18.8 Matthew Umstead, "W.Va. teacher accused of sexual assault of student," Herald-Mail Media, July 7, 2014 [Last accessed on 27 December 2014 at http://www.heraldmailmedia.com/news/tri_state/west_virgini a/w-va-teacher-accused-of-sexual-assault-of-student/article_eebbab87-d406-5148-bc2f-ad9a31291d2e.html].

18.9 Matthew Umstead, "Ex-W.Va. teacher indicted in student sex assault," Herald-Mail Media, October 21, 2014 [

Last accessed on 27 December 2014 at http://www.heraldmailmedia.com/news/tri_state/west_virgini a/ex-w-va-teacher-indicted-in-student-sex-assault/article_14cd2a4a-8678-5cdf-9522-5903c0324742.html].

18.10 Joseph Markman and Michele Morgan Bolton, "Brockton teacher charged with raping student held on $20,000 bail," *The Enterprise*, October 31, 2014 [Last accessed on 27 December 2014 at http://www.enterprisenews.com/article/20141031/NEWS/141 039075/].

18.11 Office of the District Attorney, Orange County, CA, "Anaheim High School Teacher Convicted and Sentenced for Soliciting and Possessing Photos of Underage Boys," Orange County Breeze, January 29, 2014 [Last accessed on 27 December 2014 at http://www.oc-breeze.com/2014/01/29/46649_anaheim-high-school-teacher-convicted-and-sentenced-for-soliciting-and-possessing-photos-of-underage-boys/].

19.1 At the time he was hired, the company was actually called the "Computing-Tabulating-Recording Company," (C-T-R). It was renamed as the "International Business Machines Corporation" (IBM) in 1924.

21.1 Walter Isaacson, "The Heart Wants What It Wants," *Time,* June 24, 2001 [http://content.time.com/time/magazine/article/0,9171,160439, 00.html]. In fairness, it's worth pointing out that despite the notoriety and wide-spread condemnation of the relationship, Allen and Previn have been married now for nearly 17 years.

~~~~~~~~~~

Change Log

One of the advantage of the e-book format and self-publishing is that I will be able to quickly and easily update this book in the weeks and months ahead, as new cases occur and new types of cybertraps arise. I will also be able to correct any errors that have crept in and add additional material. I hope that this book will be a living document that keeps pace with the enormous technological changes that pose such interesting and pervasive challenges to the teaching profession.

In general, minor changes to the book will be denoted by an incremental increase in the version number. Moderate changes will be marked by a jump to the next decimal, *i.e.*, from .2 to .3. Significant changes will be marked by an increase in the ordinal number, *i.e.*, from 1. to 2. The designation of version number lies in the sole discretion of the author.

Version 1.05 Reformatted the chapter and subchapter headings to make conversion to CreateSpace PDF easier; miscellaneous edits and formatting changes.

Version 1.01 7 days of additional proofreading.

Version 1.00 The original manuscript.

~~~~~~~~~

Disclaimer

General Provisions

This e-book **DOES NOT** constitute legal advice, nor does it express a legal opinion about any particular set of facts. Your purchase of this e-book does not create an attorney-client relationship with the author. If you are facing any of the situations described in this e-book, or think that any of the legal principles discussed might apply to your particular circumstances, you are STRONGLY URGED to seek professional counsel from an attorney licensed to practice law in the jurisdiction in which you reside, and in particular, to get counsel from an attorney experienced in the practice of educational law.

As the author of this e-book, I have made reasonable efforts to include accurate information regarding legislation, cases, and other legal developments; nonetheless, errors or omissions may occur. Moreover, as the law in the United States varies from state to state, and from state jurisdictions to the federal government, a correct statement of the law in one jurisdiction may not be accurate as to other jurisdictions.

To the best of my ability, the material contained in this e-book is accurate as of the date of publication. However, the law continually changes, as new legislation is passed and new decisions are handed down by the courts. You are advised that despite my best efforts, the information contained in this e-book may be out of date. I have no legal obligation to revise or update this e-book, although I may choose to do so. In the event that this e-book is updated, subsequent editions will be so identified.

The purpose of this e-book is to provide general information on the topics herein and to communicate my personal opinions and experience with respect to fascinating issues raised by the emergence of new technologies in our society.

No Warranty

I make no warranty as to either (a) the content of this e-book or (b) good results stemming from your reliance on any of the information or opinions expressed in this e-book. I specifically disclaim any liability resulting from reliance on the contents of this e-book during the course of litigation or criminal prosecution. Readers are emphatically advised that they should consult with a knowledgeable and experienced attorney licensed to practice in their jurisdiction prior to taking any action which might affect their legal rights and responsibilities.

Limitation of Liability

To the fullest extent possible by law, my total liability to you, the reader, shall not exceed the amount paid by you (or paid on behalf of you) to purchase this e-book. This limitation of liability is reasonable, because this e-book does not constitute free legal advice for your particular legal problem(s), nor is it a substitute for hiring an attorney licensed to practice in your jurisdiction who has the appropriate experience in educational or criminal law.

Acceptance

Your purchase and use of this e-book constitutes your acceptance of the above disclaimers, absence of warranty, and limitation of liability.

~~~~~~~~~~

Feedback Appreciated

Thank you for purchasing this e-book and for taking the time to read it. If you have any suggestions for ways it can be improved, or additional resources that should be added, please contact me through one of the services listed below.

Word of mouth is a huge help in promoting any book or product. If you found this guide useful, please tell your friends and acquaintances about it on your various social networks or by email.

Thank you!!

~~~~~~~~

Frederick S. Lane

About the Author

I am an author, attorney, expert witness, and professional speaker on the legal and cultural implications of emerging technology. After graduating from Amherst College and Boston College Law School, I clerked for two years for the Honorable Frank H. Freedman, Chief Judge of the U.S. District Court in Massachusetts. After practicing law for five years and writing my first book, *Vermont Jury Instructions— Civil and Criminal* [with John Dinse and Ritchie Berger] (Butterworths 1993), I launched a computer consulting business that in turn led to my current work as an author, lecturer, and computer forensics expert.

In response to the passage of the Communications Decency Act in 1996, I began researching the legislative and media response to the rise of the online adult industry. The resulting book, *Obscene Profits: The Entrepreneurs of Pornography in the Cyber Age* (Routledge 2000), was the first of what are now six mainstream non-fiction books. The others are:

- *The Naked Employee: How Technology Is Compromising Workplace Privacy* (Amacom 2003);

- *The Decency Wars: The Campaign to Cleanse American Culture* (Prometheus Books 2006);

- *The Court and the Cross: The Religious Right's Crusade to Reshape the Supreme Court* (Beacon Press 2008);

- *American Privacy: The 400-Year History of Our Most Contested Right* (Beacon Press 2010); and, most recently,

- *Cybertraps for the Young* (NTI Upstream 2011).

I have also written numerous magazine and newspaper articles on a wide variety of topics, including constitutional rights (particularly freedom of speech), privacy online and in the workplace, the impact of technology on our rights and liberties, and the separation of church and state.

On August 23, 2006, I had the honor of appearing on "The Daily Show with Jon Stewart" to discuss *The Decency Wars: The Campaign to Cleanse American Culture*. I have also appeared as a guest on a variety of other national television programs, including ABC's "Good Morning America Weekend," NBC's "Weekend Today," ABC's "Nightline," CBS's "60 Minutes," and assorted BBC documentaries. In addition to those televised appearances, I have been interviewed by numerous radio shows, magazines, and newspapers around the world on topics relating to my books.

Over the last fifteen years, I have frequently been invited to lecture before college, university, and professional audiences on topics related to my book, including Internet technology, workplace and personal privacy, computer forensics, free speech, and censorship.

~~~~~~~~

Connect With Frederick Lane Online

Via Email: FSLane3@gmail.com

On LinkedIn: Frederick Lane

On Facebook: Fred Lane

On Twitter: @Cybertraps

At FrederickLane.com

~~~~~~~~~

CPSIA information can be obtained
at www.ICGtesting.com
Printed in the USA
LVHW010524290820
664472LV00012B/1007